Fifteen-Minute
FEASTS

Fifteen-Minute
FEASTS

Lesley Waters

BBC BOOKS

Published by BBC Books
A division of BBC Enterprises Limited
Woodlands, 80 Wood Lane
London W12 0TT

First published 1991
Copyright © 1991 Lesley Waters
Line illustrations © 1991 Peter Bailey
ISBN 0 563 36198 0

Set in Itek Goudy
by Ace Filmsetting Ltd, Frome, Somerset
Printed and bound in Great Britain by Clays Ltd, St Ives Plc
Cover printed by Clays Ltd, St Ives Plc

CONTENTS

ACKNOWLEDGEMENTS

I would like to thank Erica Griffiths for sowing the seeds for *Fifteen-Minute Feasts* and her support throughout.

For painstaking work I would like to give my very special thanks to my sister Jacky, without whom this book would not have been possible.

Thanks also go to Christine Shevlen and Teresa Waite for all their patience and hard work in helping to produce this book. And last but not least to Tim and Caroline for being faithful guinea pigs.

Introduction

This book is dedicated to *Bazaar* viewers who I'm sure all love good, healthy food but don't want to spend a fortune on ingredients or hours in the kitchen. The aim of *Fifteen-Minute Feasts* is to persuade you that you don't need those pre-packed convenience meals and takeaways, and to get you back into the kitchen having fun creating delicious feasts that won't be a burden on your time. All the recipes are simple to follow and require no special skills – how often have you been put off by long complicated recipes, full of cooking waffle? I think we all have at one time or another.

This book will give you lots of ideas and useful hints and tips to guide you in the right direction. For those of you who like to ring the changes, variations are given throughout the book, as well as step-by-step time plans, approximate costs and shopping lists, so you can't go wrong. There is also a useful guide to what you need in your larder so you can always put together something quick and tasty.

Quick fifteen-minute puddings and baking recipes feature in the final two chapters of the book. These recipes have been kept separate as they are not fifteen-minute feasts but fifteen-minute recipes from start to finish. All recipes and feasts will feed at least four people and are bursting with health-giving ingredients.

Whatever the occasion – whether you're cooking for yourself, your family or for a fun supper party – this book will give you plenty of imaginative ideas. Remember, simplicity is the true recipe for success. Food isn't just a necessity or a chore, it's the centrepiece of our social lives and should be shared and enjoyed by us all – so good luck, good health and good eating.

A WORD ON NUTRITION

Simply, what you put in is what you get out! Here are a few tips to guide you towards a healthier way of eating.

1   Spend a little time on menu planning to make sure your meals are well balanced and varied. The best diet includes the whole range of food types from proteins and carbohydrates to vitamins and minerals. Variety is more fun, too.

2   Make time for your meals. Skipping meals can lead to an unhealthy diet, especially if you rely on quick snacks. Many bought snack foods are high in fat, sugar and salt – none of which is good for you in large quantities.

3   Try using wholegrain products – wholegrain pasta, rice, flour, oats, pearl barley and wheatgerm – these are good energy and fibre providers.

4   Cut down on fat – remember, less fat equals less fat! Change from whole milk to skimmed or semi- skimmed milk, cut down on foods such as cakes, biscuits and sausages which are high in fat, and try to change to low fat products wherever possible.

5   When frying, use oil sparingly. Add just enough to grease the pan and wipe out excess with kitchen paper.

6   Choose lean meat and cut down on the amount of meat you eat. You don't need to use it as the main part of the meal, or eat it every day. If you don't fancy vegetarian meals, eat more chicken and fish instead of red meats.

7   Gradually cut down on your salt – too much salt contributes to high blood pressure. I do not use salt in cooking. If you prefer to add salt to some recipes, that is up to you, but do try to cut down gradually. You will soon get used to the real taste of the food and will also reduce nutrient loss while cooking.

8   Eat lots of different fruits and vegetables for roughage and because they are packed with vitamins and minerals. You don't always need to peel vegetables; most of the time a good wash and scrub will do. Eat raw vegetables as often as possible in salads.

9   You retain more vitamins and minerals in foods if they are handled correctly.
   •   When cooking, use as little water as possible. Steam them rather than boiling so the goodness does not drain away with the water.
   •   Cook for the shortest possible time to retain nutrients, texture, flavour and colour.
   •   Don't keep food warm before it's eaten – again, it loses its nutritional value.
   •   Don't throw away vegetable water, it has goodness and flavour – use it for your gravies or keep it for vegetable stock.
   •   Try not to buy vegetables in bulk as they tend to lose a lot of nutrients during storage.

10 Choose fruits and vegetables which are in season; that way they are at their best and cheapest.

11 Pumpkin, sunflower, poppy and sesame seeds are all rich in minerals. Try them as snacks, on bread or cakes and in salads.

12 Pulses – dried beans, peas and lentils – are a great source of protein and are very cheap. Experiment with some of the different recipes in the book.

13 Cut down on refined sugar – the body simply does not need it. That means fewer cakes, biscuits and sugary snacks. Watch for 'hidden' sugar, in canned vegetables, for example, and substitute naturally sweet foods, such as fruits, when you need to sweeten recipes. If you put some raisins in your muesli and a fresh sliced banana on top, it will be as sweet as if you'd added sugar and you gain additional nutrients. The fruit sugars are absorbed more slowly by the body and aren't just empty calories.

14 Drink plenty of healthy liquids such as mineral water, herb teas, coffee substitutes and fresh fruit and vegetable juices. The body needs fluids to function efficiently.

FIFTEEN-MINUTE FEASTS
LARDER

Larders may sound old-fashioned, but if kept well stocked they make life much easier in the kitchen. A well-stocked larder or store is an easy way of providing food, and will help you plan your fifteen-minute feasts without too much shopping. To build up your store, just buy one or two extra items each week and you will soon have a well-stocked cupboard without a large single outlay.

Here is the list of the fifteen-minute larder guide. You can obviously add your own particular handy favourites.

GRAIN AND BAKING PRODUCTS

Cornflour

Bicarbonate of soda

Wholemeal, plain and self-raising flour

Porridge oats

Vanilla essence

Cocoa powder

Dried pasta: Chinese egg noodles, pasta shapes, wholemeal spaghetti, tagliatelli, vermicelli

Rice

Cracked wheat

NUTS, FRUITS AND SEEDS

Desiccated coconut

Dried fruits: apricots, figs, prunes, raisins, sultanas

Nuts: almonds, flaked almonds, hazelnuts, peanuts

Seeds: poppy, pumpkin, sesame, sunflower

SAUCES

Mint sauce

Soy sauce

Tabasco sauce

Tikka or tandoori paste

Tomato ketchup

Tomato purée

Worcestershire sauce

JUICES

Bottled lemon juice

Orange juice

SPICES AND FLAVOURINGS

Black peppercorns
Chilli sauce
Garlic purée and garlic salt
Dried herbs: basil, bay leaf, dill
  weed, mixed herbs, majoram,
  oregano, parsley, thyme
English and grainy mustard

Dried spices: cayenne pepper,
  chilli powder, ground
  cinnamon, ground coriander,
  curry powder, garam masala,
  ground ginger, ground mixed
  spice, ground nutmeg, paprika,
  turmeric
Vegetable stock cubes

SUGAR AND HONEY

Brown sugar
Honey

Maple syrup

TINNED GOODS

Beans and pulses (14 oz/400 g
  tins): borlotti beans, black-
  eyed beans, beans in tomato
  sauce, butter beans, chick peas,
  flageolet beans, kidney beans
Fruit in natural juice: keep a few
  of your favourites

Cooked brown rice
Sweetcorn
Sieved tomatoes in tins or
  cartons
Tomatoes and chopped tomatoes

MISCELLANEOUS

Dried wholemeal breadcrumbs
Eggs
Sunflower margarine or butter
Semi-skimmed milk, or whole
  milk for children

Dried milk powder
Muesli
Crunchy peanut butter
Sunflower oil

When you come to the feasts, you will see that I have not listed larder
ingredients in the shopping lists.

NOTES ON THE RECIPES

▶ PRICE GUIDE FOR EACH FEAST

Your time and your health are very valuable, of course, but the cost of recipes is important too. All the feasts in the book are designed with this in mind, and even the most exotic will not have you dipping too far into your pocket. Each feast is coded to give you an idea of how much it will cost you to make it for four people.

£	under £2.00
£££	under £4.00
£££££	under £6.00

▶ SHOPPING LISTS

The shopping lists are designed to save you time checking the ingredients for the various recipes in the feast. For convenience, items are listed in 'shops' or departments at the supermarket: butcher, greengrocer, grocer, freezer shop, baker, delicatessen. The lists do not include larder ingredients. The individual recipes later in the book do not have shopping lists as you can see the ingredients at a glance.

▶ TIME PLANS

The time plans will give you brief, at-a-glance notes on how to organise your fifteen-minute feasts. Look at them before you start and follow the sequence for maximum efficiency and speed! The full details of how to do the recipes are in the recipe method.

▶ INGREDIENTS

1   All the recipes and feasts serve four unless otherwise indicated.
2   Spoon measurements are level.
3   Eggs are size 2.
4   Do not mix metric and imperial measurements; follow one set only.

▶ KITCHEN UTENSILS

I'm not listing any kitchen equipment as these recipes do not call for sophisticated or expensive gadgets like microwaves, food processors or whatever. The only piece of electrical equipment I presume you already have is the ever-useful liquidiser. Of course, if you find you can save even more time by using your favourite gadgets – go ahead!

SOUPS FIT FOR A FEAST

PEASANT PEA SOUP WITH ITALIAN TOASTS

This nourishing and thick soup has been derived from a classic French dish with the simple addition of brown rice. However, left-over pasta or noodles may be used instead.

Serves 4   £££

SHOPPING LIST

1 onion
1 round lettuce
4 tomatoes
8 oz (225 g) frozen peas
1 small brown French stick
2 oz (50 g) Cheddar cheese

TIME PLAN

1   Follow stage 1 of soup recipe.
2   Pre-heat the grill, make mustard and cheese mix and slice tomatoes. Assemble toasts and place under grill.
3   Add rice to soup and taste for seasoning.
4   Serve soup and Italian toasts.

► PEASANT PEA SOUP

1 onion, peeled and grated
2 teaspoons garlic purée
8 oz (225 g) frozen peas
1 round lettuce, washed and shredded
2 teaspoons dried oregano

1½ pints (900 ml) vegetable stock
freshly ground black pepper
1 × 8-oz (225-g) tin cooked brown rice

1   Place the onion, garlic purée, frozen peas, lettuce and oregano in a large saucepan. Pour in the stock and season with black pepper. Cover and bring to a rapid boil, then simmer for 10 minutes.
2   Stir in the wholemeal rice. Taste and adjust the seasoning if necessary.
3   Ladle the soup into warm soup bowls and serve with Italian toasts.

▶ ITALIAN TOASTS

4 thick slices brown French bread, cut on a slant
2 oz (50 g) Cheddar cheese, grated
1 tablespoon French mustard
1 teaspoon dried mixed herbs
4 tomatoes, thinly sliced
sunflower oil for brushing
freshly ground black pepper

1   Pre-heat the grill.
2   Toast one side of the bread slices. In a small bowl, mix together the cheese, mustard, herbs and freshly ground black pepper.
3   Spread the untoasted sides of the bread with the cheese and mustard mixture.
4   Lay the tomato slices on the mixture, lightly brush with sunflower oil and grind over some black pepper.
5   Place under the grill for about 2 to 3 minutes.

ORIENTAL SOUP WITH SESAME AND POPPY SEED CRACKERS

A symphony of flavours! This soup is simple to make – a feast with an oriental theme.

Serves 4   £££££

SHOPPING LIST

4 oz (100 g) spring greens or cabbage
1 small bunch fresh parsley
1 × 8-oz (225-g) tin crab or prawns
½ packet cream cracker biscuits
4 oz (100 g) frozen mixed vegetables

TIME PLAN

1 Follow soup recipe to the end of stage 2.
2 Pre-heat the grill.
3 Prepare crackers.
4 Add noodles and fish to soup, clear decks.
5 Toast crackers and serve feast.

► ORIENTAL SOUP

8 oz (225 g) frozen mixed vegetables
4 oz (100 g) spring greens or cabbage, shredded
1 pint (600 ml) vegetable stock
5 fl oz (150 ml) orange juice
1 × 14-oz (400-g) tin chopped tomatoes

2 tablespoons soy sauce
2 teaspoons ground ginger
2 teaspoons runny honey
2 oz (50 g) Chinese egg noodles
1 × 8-oz (225-g) tin crab or prawns
2 tablespoons roughly chopped fresh parsley

1 In a large saucepan, mix together the frozen mixed vegetables, shredded greens or cabbage, stock, orange juice, tinned tomatoes, soy sauce, ginger and honey.
2 Cover and bring to a rapid boil, then simmer for 8 minutes.
3 Add the Chinese noodle and crab or prawns, and simmer for a further 5 minutes.
4 Ladle into warm soup bowls and scatter with chopped parsley.

Variation
You can omit the fish or use some cooked chicken as an alternative.

► **SESAME AND POPPY SEED CRACKERS**

½ packet of cream cracker
  biscuits

milk for brushing
sesame and poppy seeds

1   Pre-heat the grill.
2   Lightly brush the crackers with milk and scatter with the sesame and
    poppy seeds.
3   Place the crackers, seeds up, under the grill and toast for 30 seconds or
    until the seeds are lightly toasted.
4   Serve hot with oriental soup.

Salad Soup with Ham and Sweetcorn Baps

Apricot Compote

I can understand your initial reaction to cold salad soup! However, this tasty combination of refreshing ingredients makes a lovely summer feast, which you can follow with apricot compote.

Serves 4   £££££

SHOPPING LIST

2 carrots
½ cucumber
1 punnet mustard and cress
3 tomatoes
2 radishes
2 bananas
1 × 14-oz (400-g) tin apricot halves in natural juice
5 fl oz (150 ml) carrot or orange juice
2 wholemeal baps
4 slices lean ham
4 oz (100 g) low fat cream cheese
1 pint (600 ml) natural yoghurt

TIME PLAN

1 Follow baps recipe and place baps in oven.
2 Follow stage 1 of soup recipe.
3 Prepare compote and cover.
4 Remove baps from oven. Garnish and serve the soup with baps.
5 Bake compote and serve when ready.

► SALAD SOUP

1 pint (600 ml) natural yoghurt
5 fl oz (150 ml) carrot or orange juice
½ cucumber, grated
2 teaspoons garlic purée
3 teaspoons mint sauce
freshly ground black pepper

For the garnish
1 punnet mustard and cress, washed
3 tomatoes, chopped
2 radishes, sliced

1   In a large bowl, mix all the soup ingredients together. Season to taste with black pepper and pour into chilled soup bowls.
2   Scatter over the garnish and serve.

► HAM AND SWEETCORN BAPS

4 oz (100 g) low fat cream cheese
4 slices lean ham, diced
1 × 7-oz (200-g) tin sweetcorn, drained

freshly ground black pepper
2 teaspoons French mustard
2 wholemeal baps, split in half

1   Pre-heat the oven to 400°F (200°C), gas mark 6.
2   In a small bowl, beat together the cream cheese, diced ham and sweetcorn. Season with black pepper and the French mustard.
3   Fill the split baps with the filling, place baps on a baking tray and bake for 10 minutes.

► APRICOT COMPOTE

1 × 14-oz (400-g) tin apricot halves in natural juice
2 bananas, sliced

4 oz (100 g) sultanas or raisins
1 teaspoon ground cinnamon

1   Pre-heat the oven to 400°F (200°C), gas mark 6.
2   In an ovenproof dish, mix together the apricots, bananas, sultanas and cinnamon.
3   Cover with a lid or kitchen foil and bake for 10 to 15 minutes until hot and bubbling.

DEVILLED MUSHROOM SOUP WITH TACO DIP

When you're shopping, look out for the large flat mushrooms – these without a doubt have a far better flavour. When preparing your mushrooms remember that most of the flavour will come from the stalks, so try not to be too wasteful when preparing.

Serves 4   £££

SHOPPING LIST

8 oz (225 g) mushrooms
¼ cucumber
2 tomatoes
1 onion
1 packet taco chips
6 oz (175 g) frozen mixed
  peppers
granary bread
10 fl oz (300 ml) natural set
  yoghurt

TIME PLAN

1 Follow stages 1 and 2 of soup recipe.
2 Prepare dip and serve with taco chips.
3 Lay table and prepare granary bread.
4 Clear decks.
5 Taste soup for seasoning and serve feast.

▶ ## DEVILLED MUSHROOM SOUP

8 oz (225 g) mushrooms,
  chopped
1 medium onion, grated
2 heaped teaspoons ground
  coriander
1 teaspoon chilli powder
2 teaspoons paprika
1 teaspoon garlic purée
  (optional)

1 × 14-oz (400-g) tin kidney
  beans in chilli sauce
1 × 14-oz (400-g) tin chopped
  tomatoes
6 oz (175 g) frozen mixed
  peppers
15 fl oz (450 ml) water
freshly ground black pepper
granary bread, cut into chunks

1 In a large saucepan, dry fry over a high heat the mushrooms, grated onion, spices and garlic purée, if using, for approximately 2 minutes, stirring frequently.

20

2   Add the kidney beans, tinned tomatoes, peppers and water, and season well with black pepper. Cover and bring to the boil, then simmer rapidly for 7 minutes.

3   Taste and adjust the seasoning, adding extra water if necessary.

4   Ladle the soup into warm soup bowls and serve with chunks of granary bread.

► TACO DIP

10 fl oz (300 ml) natural set   2 tomatoes, chopped
   yoghurt   freshly ground black pepper
2 teaspoons mint sauce   garlic purée to taste (optional)
¼ cucumber, washed and grated   1 packet taco chips

Simply mix together all the ingredients for the dip, season to taste with black pepper and spoon into a serving dish. Place on a large plate and surround with taco chips.

Variation
Warmed pitta bread cut into fingers or vegetable crudités make a good alternative to taco chips.

BLACK-EYED BEAN SOUP WITH GARLIC TOAST SALAD

This heart-warming soup served with the garlic toast salad makes a filling feast for either lunch or supper.

Serves 4   £££

SHOPPING LIST

1 bunch spring onions
2 punnets mustard and cress
½ round lettuce
2 large oranges
6 oz (175 g) fresh or frozen
  runner beans
4 slices wholemeal or granary
  bread

TIME PLAN

1 Follow stages 1 and 2 of soup recipe.
2 Follow stages 1 and 2 of garlic toast recipe.
3 Prepare salad, adjust soup for seasoning.
4 Finish garlic toast and serve with salad and soup.

▶ BLACK-EYED BEAN SOUP

1 × 14-oz (400-g) tin black-eyed
  beans, drained
1 × 1¼-lb (500-g) carton sieved
  tomatoes
2 teaspoons garlic purée
1 bunch spring onions, chopped

6 oz (175 g) fresh or frozen
  runner beans
2 teaspoons dried thyme
15 fl oz (450 ml) vegetable stock
freshly ground black pepper

1 Place the black-eyed beans, sieved tomatoes, garlic purée, spring onions, runner beans and thyme in a large saucepan.
2 Pour in the stock and season with black pepper. Cover the pan, bring the contents to a rapid boil, then simmer for 12 minutes.
3 Taste and adjust the seasoning if necessary before serving.

Variation
To ring the changes, all types of tinned beans can be used – try borlotti, flageolet or kidney beans, for example.

▶ GARLIC TOAST SALAD

4 thick slices wholemeal or
  granary bread
1 tablespoon garlic purée
1 tablespoon sunflower oil
2 large oranges

2 punnets mustard and cress,
  washed
½ round lettuce, washed, torn
  into bite-size pieces
freshly ground black pepper

1   Pre-heat the grill and toast one side of the bread.
2   In a small bowl, mix together the garlic purée and sunflower oil, then
    spread the mixture over the untoasted side of the bread. Set to one
    side.
3   Peel the oranges and cut into thin rounds, using a sharp knife.
4   Toss the orange slices, juice, cress and lettuce together. Season with
    black pepper and serve in a large shallow dish.
5   Place the bread under the grill until golden brown (about 30 seconds).
6   Cut into wedges and place around the salad.
7   Serve at once.

CARIBBEAN FEAST

This hot and spicy feast will certainly tingle your taste buds.

Serves 4   £££

SHOPPING LIST

12 oz (350 g) potatoes
8 oz (225 g) broccoli florets
1 × 14-oz (400-g) tin pineapple
  chunks in natural juice
4 wholemeal muffins
4 oz (100 g) lean ham
10 fl oz (300 ml) fromage frais

TIME PLAN

1   Follow stages 1 and 2 of soup
    recipe (overleaf).
2   Pre-heat the grill and toast
    muffins.
3   While muffins are toasting,
    prepare pineapple pudding.
4   Place pineapple under grill.
5   Clear decks, add ham to
    soup, taste for seasoning and
    serve.
6   Serve pineapple when ready.

► CARIBBEAN SOUP

2 oz (50 g) desiccated coconut
15 fl oz (450 ml) semi-skimmed
milk
15 fl oz (450 ml) vegetable stock
12 oz (350 g) potatoes, washed
and peeled
1 tablespoon dried parsley
1 teaspoon chilli powder

1 teaspoon garlic purée
(optional)
8 oz (225 g) broccoli florets
freshly ground black pepper
4 oz (100 g) lean ham, cut into
strips
4 wholemeal muffins, split into
halves

1   In a large saucepan, mix together the coconut, milk and vegetable stock. Cover and place over a high heat. Grate the potatoes and add to the boiling milk.
2   Add the parsley, chilli powder, garlic purée, if using, and broccoli florets. Season with black pepper and stir well. Cover and bring to the boil, then simmer rapidly for 10 minutes.
3   Toast the muffins.
4   Stir in the ham, taste and adjust the seasoning, ladle into warm soup bowls and sprinkle with freshly ground black pepper to serve.

Variations
1   Curry powder can be used as an alternative to chilli.
2   Use 3 oz (75 g) grated creamed coconut instead of the desiccated coconut for a delicious alternative texture.

► CARIBBEAN PINEAPPLE PUDDING

1 × 14-oz (400-g) tin pineapple
chunks in natural juice
4 oz (100 g) porridge oats

2 teaspoons mixed spice
2 oz (50 g) brown sugar
10 fl oz (300 ml) fromage frais

1   Pre-heat the grill.
2   Place the pineapple chunks with half the juice in a flameproof dish.
3   In a small bowl, mix together the oats, mixed spice and brown sugar.
4   Scatter the oat mixture over the pineapple chunks and place under the grill for 4 to 5 minutes until golden brown.
5   Serve straight away with fromage frais.

Variation
For an even quicker topping, scatter the pineapple with breakfast muesli.

GRAIN AND PASTA FEASTS

SOUTH CAROLINA FEAST

This filling, comforting feast is great for a chilly winter day. Any left-over rice can be used, but wholegrain rice is best as it's a good source of fibre and vitamin B. You can now buy cooked brown rice in tins.

Serves 4   £££

SHOPPING LIST

1 bunch spring onions
4 large carrots
1 bunch watercress
granary bread
4 oz (100 g) salami
5 fl oz (150 ml) fromage frais or
   natural yoghurt

TIME PLAN

1 Follow stage 1 of Carolina rice recipe.
2 Prepare carrot ribbons and make salad dressing (overleaf).
3 Toss salad with dressing.
4 Taste rice and adjust seasoning.
5 Clear decks and serve South Carolina feast.

▶ **CAROLINA RICE**

2 teaspoons garlic purée
1 bunch spring onions, chopped
4 oz (100 g) salami, cut into
   strips
1 × 14-oz (400-g) tin black-eyed
   beans, drained
1 × 7-oz (200-g) tin sweetcorn,
   drained

2 × 10-oz (275-g) tins cooked
   brown rice
1 bayleaf
½ teaspoon cayenne pepper
freshly ground black pepper
1 pint (600 ml) vegetable stock

1   In a large saucepan, dry fry the garlic purée, spring onions and salami strips for 30 seconds. Add the remaining ingredients, cover, bring to the boil, then simmer rapidly for 10 minutes. It may be necessary to add more stock during cooking.
2   Taste and adjust the seasoning if necessary. Spoon the rice into a large serving dish or serve straight from the saucepan with large chunks of granary bread.

Variations
1   Left-over cooked pasta can be used as a substitute for rice.
2   To ring the changes try using different types of tinned beans, such as flageolet, borlotti, chick peas.
3   Cold ham or cooked chicken makes a good alternative to salami.

► **CARROT RIBBON SALAD**

4 large carrots, peeled
1 bunch watercress, washed and
   picked

Seedy pasta feast dressing (see
   page 28)
freshly ground black pepper

1   Using a swivel peeler, continue peeling the carrots into ribbon strips or simply just grate the carrots.
2   In a salad bowl, toss the carrot ribbons with the watercress and dressing, and season to taste with black pepper.

SEEDY PASTA FEAST

Pasta is always a favourite of mine because of its simplicity. This unusual combination of pasta and seeds makes a delicious and nourishing dish.

Serves 4   £££

SHOPPING LIST

4 large tomatoes
1 medium Spanish onion
1 punnet mustard and cress
1 × 14-oz (400-g) tin pimentoes
granary bread
5 fl oz (150 ml) fromage frais or
  natural yoghurt

TIME PLAN

1   Follow stages 1 and 2 of pasta recipe.
2   Prepare salad (overleaf) and arrange on serving dish.
3   Make salad dressing, prepare bread and clear decks.
4   Drain and finish pasta recipe.
5   Spoon dressing over salad and serve feast.

► SUPER SEEDY PASTA

14 oz (400 g) wholemeal pasta
  shapes
1 teaspoon poppy seeds
1 × 14-oz (400-g) tin pimentoes,
  drained and sliced

1 tablespoon sunflower oil
1 teaspoon garlic purée
freshly ground black pepper
4 oz (100 g) sunflower seeds
4 oz (100 g) pumpkin seeds

1   Tip the pasta shapes into a large saucepan of boiling water, cover with a lid and boil for 8 to 10 minutes.
2   In a small saucepan, dry fry the poppy seeds until lightly roasted. Add the sliced pimentoes, oil, garlic purée, black pepper, sunflower seeds and pumpkin seeds. Set to one side.
3   Drain the pasta well and return it to the saucepan, spoon in the pimento mixture and toss. Season to taste with black pepper and serve.

Variations
1   All different types of pasta can be used.
2   I like to dry fry the sunflower seeds in soy sauce before using them, as this gives them a lovely flavour.

▶ TOMATO, ONION AND CRESS SALAD

4 large tomatoes, thinly sliced
1 medium Spanish onion, thinly
   sliced
1 punnet mustard and cress,
   washed

For the dressing
5 fl oz (150 ml) fromage frais or
   natural yoghurt
2 tablespoons orange juice
1 teaspoon runny honey
2 teaspoons dill weed

freshly ground black pepper
granary bread

1   Arrange slices of tomato and onion on a large plate.
2   Scatter over the mustard and cress.
3   In a small bowl, mix together the dressing ingredients. Season well
    with black pepper to taste, then trickle the dressing over the salad.
4   Serve with chunks of granary bread.

SPAGHETTI SATAY WITH COS AND CUCUMBER PLATTER

ORANGE COOLERS

This feast is based on an Indonesian idea, using pasta instead of rice. The combination of peanut butter and coconut sauce marries perfectly with the simple cos platter.

Serves 4   £££

SHOPPING LIST

4 oz (100 g) bacon
2 courgettes
½ cos lettuce
½ cucumber
4 large oranges

TIME PLAN

1   Follow stages 1 and 2 of spaghetti satay recipe.
2   Prepare oranges (overleaf), chill or freeze.
3   Arrange lettuce and cucumber on platter (overleaf).
4   Drain and serve spaghetti with satay sauce and cos platter.
5   To finish, clear your palate with the refreshing orange coolers.

▶ SPAGHETTI SATAY

1 lb (450 g) wholewheat
  spaghetti
4 oz (100 g) bacon, diced
2 courgettes, chopped
1 × 14-oz (400-g) tin chopped
  tomatoes
3 oz (75 g) peanut butter

1 tablespoon desiccated coconut
1 teaspoon dried mixed herbs
2 tablespoons soy sauce
2 tablespoons lemon juice
½ teaspoon chilli powder
1 teaspoon garlic purée
10 fl oz (300 ml) water

29

1   Place the spaghetti in a large pan of boiling water, cover and boil for 12 minutes.
2   Dry fry the diced bacon and courgettes for 2 minutes. Add the remaining ingredients, stir and cook for 8 minutes.
3   Drain the spaghetti and divide between four plates or bowls, ladle over the piping hot satay sauce.

Variation
Creamed coconut is now available in most supermarkets and gives a delicious texture to the sauce. Use 2 oz (50 g) grated creamed coconut instead of the desiccated coconut if you prefer.

▶ COS AND CUCUMBER PLATTER

½ cos lettuce   1 tablespoon lemon juice
½ cucumber   freshly ground black pepper

1   Arrange large leaves of cos lettuce with the cucumber slices on a large plate or platter.
2   Sprinkle over the lemon juice and freshly ground black pepper.

▶ ORANGE COOLERS

4 large oranges

1   Cut each orange into 6 wedges.
2   Place the orange wedges on a large plate and chill, or better still freeze, for 10 minutes.

COSMOPOLITAN COUS COUS

CHILLED BLACK GRAPES

Cous cous is a coarsely ground hard wheat which has been pre-cooked so the preparation is easy. You can flavour cous cous with nuts, seeds, dried fruits or spices – the variations are endless. The chilled black grapes offer a simple but perfect way to finish your Eastern-style feast.

Serves 4   £££

SHOPPING LIST

1 small bunch fresh parsley
3 tomatoes
1 lb (450 g) black grapes
1 medium onion
1 lb (450 g) cous cous
1 × 14-oz (400-g) tin chopped tomatoes
12 oz (350 g) frozen green beans

TIME PLAN

1   Soak cous cous.
2   Wash and chill grapes.
3   Follow stages 1 to 3 of cous cous recipe.
4   Clear decks, divide grapes into small bunches and place on ice, return to the refrigerator.
5   Heat and fluff up cous cous, add the pumpkin seeds and chopped parsley.
6   Taste and season vegetables if necessary, then serve feast.

▶ COSMOPOLITAN COUS COUS

1 lb (450 g) cous cous
1 medium onion, grated
2 teaspoons garlic purée
1 × 14-oz (400-g) tin chopped tomatoes
3 tomatoes, chopped
12 oz (350 g) frozen green beans
freshly ground black pepper

1 teaspoon dried thyme
1 teaspoon brown sugar
1 tablespoon Worcestershire sauce
1 bay leaf
1 small bunch fresh parsley, chopped
3 oz (75 g) pumpkin seeds

1   Place the cous cous in a large bowl and allow it to soak in 1 pint (600 ml) of water for 10 minutes.
2   In a large saucepan, dry fry the grated onion and garlic purée for 1 minute.
3   Add the tinned and chopped tomatoes, green beans, black pepper, thyme, sugar, Worcestershire sauce and bay leaf. Cover, bring to the boil and simmer rapidly for 10 minutes.
4   Heat and fluff up the cous cous in a large saucepan over a gentle heat for 3 to 4 minutes. Stir half the chopped parsley, the pumpkin seeds and some black pepper into the cous cous and divide on to 4 large plates.
5   Remove the lid from the vegetables, taste and adjust seasoning and ladle over the cous cous. Scatter with the remaining chopped parsley. Serve at once.

Variations
1   Cous cous is becoming more readily available in Britain. However, if you have difficulty finding it, you can substitute cracked wheat or rice.
2   Pumpkin seeds give a crunchy texture to this dish; however, any seeds or nuts may be used.

▶ **CHILLED BLACK GRAPES**

1 lb (450 g) black grapes, washed

1   Chill the grapes in the refrigerator.
2   Divide the grapes into smaller bunches and arrange on a platter of ice.

32

CRACKED WHEAT KORMA WITH RELISH COOLERS

This is an 'instant' way of making a curry with the unusual addition of cracked wheat instead of rice. Together with the refreshing relishes, it makes a fabulous feast.

Serves 4   £££

SHOPPING LIST

2 onions
1 apple
1 large banana
3 tomatoes
1 lemon
1 × 14-oz (400-g) tin okra
4 wholemeal pitta breads
5 fl oz (150 ml) natural yoghurt

TIME PLAN

1   Follow stages 1 and 2 of cracked wheat korma recipe.
2   Clear decks.
3   Pre-heat the grill, prepare relishes, check cracked wheat.
4   Lightly toast pitta bread.
5   Serve cracked wheat with the vegetable korma and serve relishes separately.

► CRACKED WHEAT KORMA

1 lb (450 g) cracked wheat, washed
1 pint (600 ml) vegetable stock
2 slices lemon
1 bay leaf
1 tablespoon dried parsley
1 onion, grated
1 apple, chopped
3 teaspoons garam masala

1 × 14-oz (400-g) tin beans in tomato sauce
1 × 14-oz (400-g) tin chopped tomatoes
1 × 14-oz (400-g) tin okra, drained
5 fl oz (150 ml) vegetable stock
5 fl oz (150 ml) natural yoghurt
4 wholemeal pitta breads

1   Place the cracked wheat in a large saucepan and pour over the boiling stock. Add the lemon slices, bay leaf and dried parsley. Bring to the boil, cover and simmer for 10 to 12 minutes until the wheat is tender and most of the stock has been absorbed. (During cooking you may need to add extra stock.)

2   In a medium-sized saucepan, dry fry the grated onion, chopped apple and garam masala for 30 seconds. Pour in the tinned beans, tomatoes and okra. Add the vegetable stock and season well. Cover and cook for 10 minutes, stirring occasionally.

3   Divide the cracked wheat between 4 plates, ladle over the vegetable korma and dribble over the natural yoghurt.

4   Serve with the relish coolers and toasted pitta bread.

Variations

1   Fresh or tinned okra can be used for this dish.

2   Frozen runner beans can be used instead of okra if you prefer.

3   Garam masala means 'hot mixture' and is made from many spices. Curry powder can be used instead, but take care not to use too much as its flavour will dominate the whole dish.

► TOMATO, ONION AND MINT RELISH

3 tomatoes, chopped   pinch of sugar
1 onion, chopped   freshly ground black pepper
2 teaspoons mint sauce

1   Mix together the chopped tomato, onion, mint sauce and a pinch of sugar. Season to taste with black pepper and spoon into a serving pot.

► BANANA, RAISIN AND COCONUT RELISH

1 large banana, chopped   juice of ½ lemon
1 oz (25 g) desiccated coconut   freshly ground black pepper
1 oz (25 g) raisins

1   Mix together the chopped banana, desiccated coconut, raisins and lemon juice. Season well with black pepper and spoon into a serving pot.

CRACKED WHEAT KEDGEREE WITH YOGHURT COOLER

Cracked wheat, sometimes known as burghul, is a wheat that has been boiled, dried and then ground. You can serve it in place of rice or pasta and it's quick, filling and easy to use.

Serves 4   £££

SHOPPING LIST

1 large onion
1 small bunch fresh parsley
2 × 4-oz (100-g) tins smoked oysters or mussels
1 × 7-oz (200-g) tin blackcurrants or blackberries in natural juice
8 oz (225 g) frozen peas
4 wholemeal pitta breads
1 pint (600 ml) natural yoghurt
3 oz (75 g) Cheddar cheese

TIME PLAN

1   Follow stages 1 and 2 of kedgeree recipe.
2   Make yoghurt cooler and place in refrigerator to chill.
3   Clear decks, prepare garnish.
4   Add oysters or mussels to kedgeree and season to taste.
5   Scatter with the cheese and serve straight from the pan with the pitta bread and yoghurt cooler.

▶ CRACKED WHEAT KEDGEREE

1 tablespoon sunflower oil
1 large onion, grated
1 teaspoon turmeric (optional)
2 teaspoons garlic purée (optional)
2 oz (50 g) vermicelli
8 oz (225 g) cracked wheat, washed
8 oz (225 g) frozen peas
½ teaspoon ground nutmeg
1 bay leaf

15 fl oz (450 ml) vegetable stock
2 × 4-oz (100-g) tins smoked oysters or mussels, drained

For the garnish
2 oz (50 g) Cheddar cheese, grated
2 tablespoons chopped fresh parsley

4 wholemeal pitta breads

35

1   Heat the oil in a wok or large frying pan, and fry the grated onion, turmeric and garlic purée, if using, for 1 minute. Add the vermicelli and cracked wheat, and cook for 30 seconds over a high heat, stirring continuously.
2   Add all the remaining ingredients except the oysters or mussels, cover the pan and simmer for 8 to 10 minutes.
3   Fork in the oysters or mussels and scatter with the cheese and parsley garnish. Serve at once with hot pitta bread.

Variations
1   Any frozen vegetables can be used but peas lend themselves best to this dish.
2   Smoked oysters or mussels are widely available in supermarkets and give a delicious smoked flavour.

► YOGHURT COOLER

1 pint (600 ml) natural yoghurt   honey
5 fl oz (150 ml) orange juice   ground cinnamon
1 × 7-oz (200-g) tin blackcurrants
  or blackberries in natural juice

1   Liquidise the yoghurt, orange juice and blackcurrants together for 20 seconds.
2   Taste for sweetness, adding honey if necessary.
3   Pour the yoghurt drink into 4 tall glasses and place in the refrigerator to chill. A few minutes before serving, add ice and sprinkle with cinnamon.

MAIN COURSE SALADS – AND SOME TASTY SALAD DRESSINGS

CAESAR SALAD FEAST

CHILLED BLACK GRAPES

Caesar salad is a simple main salad, best served on its own to appreciate the combination of flavours and textures.

Serves 4   £ £

SHOPPING LIST

1 cos lettuce
2 punnets mustard and cress
1 lb (450 g) black grapes
1 × 7-oz (200-g) tin tuna fish in brine
4 slices granary bread
4 granary rolls
2 oz (50 g) strong Cheddar cheese

TIME PLAN

1   Chill black grapes: see page 32.
2   Follow complete Caesar salad recipe.
3   Clear decks.
4   Serve Caesar feast.
5   Serve grapes when ready.

▶ CAESAR SALAD

2 eggs
1 teaspoon garlic purée
1 teaspoon dried parsley
freshly ground black pepper
1 tablespoon sunflower oil

For the dressing
2 tablespoons lemon juice
2 teaspoons Worcestershire sauce
2 teaspoons wholegrain mustard
3 tablespoons sunflower oil
2 oz (50 g) strong Cheddar
  cheese, grated
freshly ground black pepper

4 slices granary bread
1 oz (25 g) butter
Marmite
1 cos lettuce, washed and torn
  into bite-size pieces
2 punnets mustard and cress,
  washed
1 × 7-oz (200-g) tin tuna fish in
  brine, drained
4 granary rolls

1   Pre-heat the grill.
2   Whisk the eggs, garlic purée and parsley together and season with
    black pepper.
3   Heat the oil in a frying pan, add the eggs and gently stir with a fork,
    drawing in liquid from the sides to the centre. When the eggs are set,
    stop stirring and cook for 1 minute until the bottom is set. Place the
    frying pan under the hot grill and cook for 1 minute or until firm. Set
    the omelette to one side.
4   In a mixing bowl, combine all the dressing ingredients. Season to taste
    with black pepper.
5   Toast the bread on each side and lightly spread with butter and
    Marmite. Cut each slice into 9 cubes.
6   In a large salad bowl, toss together the lettuce, mustard and cress and
    Marmite croûtons.
7   Slice the omelette into noodle-like strips and add to the salad with the
    dressing. Toss gently and flake over the drained tuna fish. Serve at
    once with warm granary rolls.

▶ CHILLED BLACK GRAPES

See recipe on page 32.

MEXICAN-STYLE SALAD FEAST

Start your feast with guacamole and taco chips, one of the most traditional
and famous Mexican dishes, followed by a hot and spicy salad.

Serves 4   £££

SHOPPING LIST

4 large tomatoes
1 large ripe avocado
1 small onion
½ cucumber
1 large green pepper
1 punnet mustard and cress
1 bunch radishes
4 wholemeal pitta breads
1 packet taco chips

TIME PLAN

1   Follow stages 1 and 2 of hot
    rice salad recipe (overleaf).
2   Follow complete guacamole
    dip recipe and set to one
    side.
3   Follow stages 3 to 5 of hot
    rice salad recipe.
4   Clear decks.
5   Serve Mexican salad feast.

▶ GUACAMOLE

4 large tomatoes, chopped
2 tablespoons lemon juice
1 small onion, grated
1 teaspoon ground coriander
1 large ripe avocado

freshly ground black pepper
chilli sauce to taste (optional)

To serve with dip
1 packet taco chips
1 bunch radishes, washed

1   Mix together the tomatoes, lemon juice, grated onion and ground
    coriander. Cut the avocado in half, scoop out the flesh and mash it
    into the tomato mixture. Season to taste with black pepper.
2   Spoon the guacamole into a serving dish, place on a large platter and
    surround with the taco chips and radishes.

▶ HOT RICE SALAD

2 × 8-oz (225-g) tins cooked
  brown rice
1 × 14-oz (400-g) tin beans in
  tomato sauce
1 × 7-oz (200-g) tin sweetcorn
1 teaspoon garlic purée
1 teaspoon chilli sauce
freshly ground black pepper

For the topping
1 punnet mustard and cress
½ cucumber, finely diced
1 large green pepper, deseeded
  and chopped
1 teaspoon paprika

4 wholemeal pitta breads

1 In a saucepan, heat the cooked rice in the water for 3 minutes, then cover.
2 In a separate saucepan, heat the beans, sweetcorn and its juice, garlic purée and chilli sauce. Season with black pepper and simmer for 4 minutes.
3 Meanwhile, prepare the topping. Add the hot bean mixture to the heated rice, mix gently and season to taste with black pepper.
4 Pile the spicy rice into a serving dish and set to one side.
5 Prepare the topping and toss together. Scatter the topping over the rice salad and serve with warm pitta bread.

Variations
1 To save washing-up time, mash your avocado halves in their skins with a fork.
2 If you like your food hot and spicy like the Mexicans, add extra chilli and garlic.

SEEDY CHICKEN AND HOT CUCUMBER SALAD WITH MUSTARD BREAD

Gone are the days of boring, limp lettuce salads. Here we have a tasty, warm salad full of sizzling sesame chicken.

Serves 4   £££

SHOPPING LIST

10 oz (275 g) boned, skinned
  chicken flesh
1 cucumber
1 cos or Webb's lettuce
1 punnet cherry tomatoes, halved
1 small brown French stick

TIME PLAN

1 Follow stages 1 and 2 of
  mustard bread recipe
  (overleaf).

2 Follow stages 1 and 2 of
  chicken and cucumber salad
  recipe.

3 Follow stage 3 of mustard
  bread recipe.

4 Follow stages 3 and 4 of
  chicken and cucumber salad
  recipe.

5 Remove mustard bread from
  grill and serve feast.

▶ SEEDY CHICKEN AND HOT CUCUMBER SALAD

½ tablespoon sunflower oil
10 oz (275 g) boned, skinned
  chicken flesh, cut into strips
freshly ground black pepper
4 teaspoons garlic purée
3 tablespoons soy sauce
2 teaspoons honey
3 tablespoons water
1 tablespoon cornflour
1 cucumber, cut into large dice
3 tablespoons sesame seeds

For the dressing
2 tablespoons lemon juice
1 teaspoon honey
1 teaspoon French mustard
2 tablespoons sunflower oil
freshly ground black pepper

1 cos or Webb's lettuce, washed
  and shredded
1 punnet cherry tomatoes, halved

1   Heat the oil in a wok or large frying pan. Season the chicken strips with black pepper, add the chicken and garlic purée to the pan and fry for 2 to 3 minutes until golden. In a small saucepan, mix together the soy sauce, honey, water and cornflour.
2   Add the cucumber to the chicken and stir-fry for a further 2 minutes. Pour in the soy sauce mixture and sesame seeds. Stir-fry for a further 1 minute, then remove from the heat and set to one side.
3   In a small bowl, mix together dressing ingredients and trickle over the lettuce and tomatoes. Toss well and divide the salad between 4 large plates.
4   Spoon the hot chicken and juices over the salad and serve at once with mustard bread.

Variations
1   Strips of cod may be used in place of chicken; however, the fish will take less time to cook.
2   Make sure your wok or frying pan is good and hot so your chicken will fry quickly and not stew and become dry.
3   If cherry tomatoes are too pricey, substitute ordinary ones and cut into small pieces.

▶ MUSTARD BREAD

1 small brown French stick
1 teaspoon garlic purée
2 tablespoons French mustard

1 oz (25 g) butter or sunflower margarine

1   Pre-heat the grill. Split the French stick in half lengthways.
2   Mix together the remaining ingredients and spread the mustard mixture over the bread.
3   Lightly toast under the grill for 1 to 2 minutes. Serve at once.

PEANUT GADO GADO SALAD

CHILLED MELON WITH GINGER

A traditional Indonesian dish, this feast uses vegetables, salad ingredients and a tasty peanut dressing.

Serves 4   £££

SHOPPING LIST

1 small cauliflower
8 oz (225 g) fresh spinach
4 oz (100 g) bean shoots
4 large carrots
3 tomatoes
2 punnets mustard and cress
1 small onion
1 honeydew melon
1 brown French stick

TIME PLAN

1   Follow stage 1 of gado gado salad.
2   Prepare melon wedges and chill in the refrigerator.
3   Follow stages 2 to 5 of gado gado salad.
4   Serve feast.
5   Serve melon when ready.

▶ PEANUT GADO GADO SALAD

1 small cauliflower, broken into florets
8 oz (225 g) fresh spinach, washed and shredded
4 oz (100 g) bean shoots
4 large carrots, grated

For the spicy peanut dressing
1 tablespoon sunflower oil
1 small onion, chopped
1 teaspoon garlic purée
1 teaspoon ground coriander
½ teaspoon chilli powder

1 teaspoon desiccated coconut
4 tablespoons crunchy peanut butter
5 fl oz (150 ml) water
1 tablespoon lemon juice
1 tablespoon soy sauce
freshly ground black pepper

For the topping
3 tomatoes, finely chopped
2 punnets mustard and cress, washed

1 brown French stick

1   Cook the cauliflower florets in boiling water for 5 to 6 minutes until just tender.
2   Meanwhile, in a large salad bowl, combine the shredded spinach, bean shoots and carrots.
3   To make the peanut dressing, heat the oil in a saucepan and gently fry the onion and garlic purée for 1 minute. Remove the saucepan from the heat and mix in the remaining dressing ingredients. Return the pan to the heat and simmer for 2 minutes, adding more water if necessary. Season to taste with black pepper.
4   Drain the cauliflower and refresh under cold running water. Add to the salad ingredients and pour over the spicy peanut dressing. Sprinkle over the topping and serve.
5   Serve with chunks of warm brown bread.

► CHILLED MELON WITH GINGER

1 honeydew melon   ground ginger

1   Cut the melon into wedges and remove the seeds with a spoon.
2   Sprinkle the melon with ground ginger and chill in the freezer for 10 minutes.

Tandoori Pasta Salad

Hot Pink Grapefruit

The combination of raisins and spices goes particularly well with the pasta.

Serves 4   £££

SHOPPING LIST

8 oz (225 g) mushrooms
2 pink grapefruit
1 red pepper
1 bunch watercress
4 wholemeal pitta breads
4 oz (100 g) lean ham
10 fl oz (300 ml) fromage frais

TIME PLAN

1   Follow stages 1 to 3 of pasta recipe.
2   Pre-heat the grill and prepare grapefruit (overleaf).
3   Warm pitta bread under grill. Place in a basket, cover with a cloth.
4   While grapefruit is grilling, drain pasta, toss salad and serve feast.
5   Serve grapefruit when ready.

▶ **TANDOORI PASTA SALAD**

1 lb (450 g) green tagliatelli or vermicelli

For the dressing
10 fl oz (300 ml) fromage frais
2 tablespoons orange juice
2 tablespoons tandoori or tikka paste
1 teaspoon garlic purée
1 tablespoon sunflower oil

3 tablespoons water
1 teaspoon mint sauce
freshly ground black pepper
8 oz (225 g) mushrooms, sliced
4 oz (100 g) lean ham
4 oz (100 g) raisins
1 red pepper, sliced

1 bunch watercress, trimmed

1   Cook the pasta in plenty of boiling water for 8 to 10 minutes.
2   In a mixing bowl, mix the dressing ingredients together. Season to taste with black pepper and set to one side.

45

3   In a large mixing bowl, toss together the mushrooms, ham, raisins and red pepper.
4   Drain the pasta and refresh under cold running water. Add the pasta to the mushroom mixture and pour over the dressing.
5   Toss well and pile into a serving dish. Scatter with watercress and serve with the warm toasted pitta breads.

Variation
There are many types of dried or fresh pasta available now, so give them a try. Any type of grapefruit may be used, but pink grapefruit lend themselves best to this recipe.

▶ HOT PINK GRAPEFRUIT

2 tablespoons brown sugar   2 pink grapefruit
1 teaspoon ground cinnamon

1   Pre-heat the grill.
2   In a small bowl, mix together the brown sugar and cinnamon.
3   Cut the grapefruit in half and, using a sharp knife, cut the flesh between the segments.
4   Spread the sugar mixture over the grapefruit halves and grill for 3 to 4 minutes or until bubbling hot.
5   Serve straight away.

TUSCANY SALAD FEAST

A delicious, filling Italian salad served with mini-mock pizzas.

Serves 4   £££

SHOPPING LIST

1 bunch spring onions
4 tomatoes
1 small onion
4 oz (100 g) black olives
  (optional)
8 oz (225 g) frozen broad beans
8 oz (225 g) frozen green beans
2 wholemeal muffins
10 fl oz (300 ml) fromage frais
4 slices salami
2 oz (50 g) strong Cheddar
  cheese

TIME PLAN

1   Pre-heat the grill.
2   Follow stages 1 to 3 of salad
    recipe.
3   Follow complete mini-pizzas
    recipe (overleaf).
4   Clear decks while pizzas are
    under grill.
5   Follow stage 4 of salad recipe.
6   Serve Tuscany salad with
    mini-pizzas.

▶ TUSCANY SALAD

8 oz (225 g) frozen broad beans
8 oz (225 g) frozen green beans
1 × 14-oz (400-g) tin butter
  beans, drained
1 × 14-oz (400-g) tin borlotti
  beans, drained

For the spring onion dressing
1 bunch spring onions, chopped
10 fl oz (300 ml) fromage frais
2 teaspoons dried oregano
2 teaspoons garlic purée
1 tablespoon sunflower oil
1 tablespoon lemon juice
freshly ground black pepper

1   In a saucepan of boiling water, cook the frozen beans for 3 minutes.
2   Meanwhile, in a large serving bowl, toss together the butter beans and
    borlotti beans.
3   In a small bowl, combine the dressing ingredients together and season
    to taste with black pepper.

4   Drain the cooked, frozen beans and refresh under running water, drain
    well and toss with the drained, tinned beans.
5   Pour over the spring onion dressing and toss well. Season with black
    pepper and serve.

▶ MINI·PIZZAS

2 wholemeal muffins, halved
4 slices salami
4 tomatoes, thinly sliced
1 small onion, grated
1 teaspoon dried oregano

4 oz (100 g) black olives, stoned
    (optional)
2 oz (50 g) strong Cheddar
    cheese, grated

1   Pre-heat the grill.
2   Toast one side of the muffins and place a slice of salami on each.
3   Top each muffin with the tomato slices and sprinkle over the grated
    onion, oregano, black olives, if using, and grated cheese.
4   Place under a hot grill for 2 to 3 minutes until bubbling hot and golden
    brown. Serve mini-pizzas at once.

Variation
Crumpets or wholemeal baps can be used in place of the muffins.

GREAT VEGETABLE FEASTS

SUNFLOWER MUSHROOM CUPS
WITH COS PLATTER AND
GRANARY BREAD

Large flat mushrooms stuffed and grilled with a delicious mixture of vegetables and sunflower seeds, topped with a little blue cheese, make a mouth-watering feast. Follow it with some fresh fruit.

Serves 4   £££

SHOPPING LIST

8 large mushrooms
2 sticks celery
3 tomatoes
½ cos lettuce
½ cucumber
choice of fresh fruit
granary bread
3 oz (75 g) blue cheese

TIME PLAN

1   Follow stages 1 to 9 of
    mushroom cup recipe
    (overleaf).
2   Clear decks and prepare cos
    platter and granary bread.
3   Arrange fresh fruit of choice.
4   Serve feast.

► SUNFLOWER MUSHROOM CUPS

8 large mushrooms, peeled
sunflower oil for brushing
freshly ground black pepper

For the stuffing
4 slices granary or wholemeal
  bread
2 sticks celery, finely chopped
3 tomatoes, finely chopped
mushroom stalks
1 teaspoon garlic purée
  (optional)

2 oz (50 g) sunflower seeds
1 egg, beaten
1 teaspoon dried marjoram
1 × 7-oz (200-g) tin sweetcorn,
  drained
freshly ground black pepper
3 oz (75 g) blue cheese, grated

granary bread
fresh fruit of your choice

1   Pre-heat the grill.
2   Remove the mushroom stalks and keep to one side.
3   Brush the mushrooms with oil and season with black pepper. Place
    on grilling tray, open side uppermost, and grill for 4 to 5 minutes.
4   Meanwhile, make the stuffing. Soak the bread in cold water for 30
    seconds and squeeze out excess water. Using your hands, pull the
    bread into small pieces and place in a mixing bowl.
5   Mix in the chopped celery, tomatoes, mushroom stalks, garlic purée,
    if using, sunflower seeds, egg, marjoram and drained sweetcorn.
6   Mash together with a fork and season well with black pepper.
7   Remove the mushrooms from the grill.
8   Fill each mushroom cup with the stuffing and scatter with cheese.
9   Place under the grill for a further 6 to 7 minutes until bubbling hot
    and golden.
10 Serve straight away with chunks of granary bread, cos and cucumber
    platter and fresh fruit of your choice.

Variations
1   Cheddar, Edam or Stilton can be used instead of blue cheese.
2   Sunflower seeds give a delicious crunchy texture; however, poppy,
    sesame or pumpkin seeds can be used instead.

► COS AND CUCUMBER PLATTER

See recipe on page 30.

VEGEDILAS WITH SWEET AND SOUR SAUCE

FRESH FRUIT SMOOTHIE

These moist burgers flavoured with hazelnuts are delicious served hot or cold. Any type of beans may be used for the vegedilas.

Serves 4   £££

SHOPPING LIST

1 bunch spring onions
2 carrots
¼ iceberg lettuce
2 bananas
4 muesli-type biscuits
4 wholemeal baps
1 pint (600 ml) natural yoghurt
   or fromage frais

TIME PLAN

1   Follow stages 1 to 5 of vegedilas recipe.
2   Prepare sweet and sour sauce.
3   Prepare lettuce for baps. Make and chill fruit smoothie.
4   Place vegedilas on lettuce-filled baps and serve with the sweet and sour sauce.
5   Sprinkle fruit smoothie with cocoa and serve with biscuits.

▶ VEGEDILAS WITH SWEET AND SOUR SAUCE

1 × 14-oz (400-g) tin chick peas, drained
4 oz (100 g) hazelnuts, chopped
1 bunch spring onions, chopped
2 carrots, grated
2 tablespoons tomato purée
1 tablespoon Worcestershire sauce

1 egg
freshly ground black pepper
dried wholemeal breadcrumbs for coating
4 wholemeal baps, split
crisp lettuce leaves

51

1   Pre-heat the grill.
2   In a large bowl, mash the drained chick peas with a potato masher or, if you haven't a masher, clench your fist and pummel the chick peas with your hand. You can use a fork but it will take a lot longer.
3   Stir in the hazelnuts, onions, carrots, tomato purée, Worcestershire sauce and egg and mix well. Season to taste with black pepper.
4   Shape the mixture into 4 flat burgers and lightly sprinkle with the breadcrumbs.
5   Grill the vegedilas for 3 to 4 minutes each side, turning carefully.
6   Lightly toast the baps and serve the vegedilas on toasted baps filled with crisp lettuce leaves.
7   Hand round the sweet and sour sauce separately.

► SWEET AND SOUR SAUCE

1 × 18-oz (500-g) carton sieved or creamed tomatoes	1 tablespoon lemon juice
	2 tablespoons soy sauce
3 tablespoons orange juice	1 teaspoon garlic purée
2 teaspoons honey	freshly ground black pepper

In a saucepan, simmer all the ingredients together for 5 minutes. Season to taste with black pepper and serve with the vegedilas.

Variation
A lovely alternative is yoghurt and mint sauce (see page 56).

► FRESH FRUIT SMOOTHIE

2 bananas	2 teaspoons honey or maple syrup
1 pint (600 ml) natural yoghurt or fromage frais	2 teaspoons cocoa powder
5 fl oz (150 ml) orange juice	4 muesli-type biscuits

1   Liquidise all the smoothie ingredients except the cocoa powder and biscuits. Place in the refrigerator.
2   Pour into glasses, sprinkle with sifted cocoa powder and serve with muesli biscuits.

Variation
Any type of soft fruit can be used for your fruit smoothie.

FLORENTINE VEGETABLE LAYER WITH CARROT AND POPPY SEED SALAD

The nutmeg gives the spinach a delicious nutty taste. If you wish you can add some smoked fish or meat to this dish.

Serves 4   £££

SHOPPING LIST

3 large beef tomatoes or 1 lb (450 g) small tomatoes
4 large carrots
1 × 14-oz (400-g) tin pimentoes
1 lb (450 g) frozen leaf spinach
1 French stick, brown or white
3 oz (75 g) strong Cheddar cheese

TIME PLAN

1 Follow stages 1 to 7 of Florentine layer recipe.
2 Prepare salad (overleaf).
3 Clear decks and serve feast.

► FLORENTINE VEGETABLE LAYER

1 lb (450 g) frozen leaf spinach
3 large beef tomatoes or 1 lb (450 g) small tomatoes, sliced
1 × 14-oz (400-g) tin red pimentoes, drained
1 tablespoon sunflower oil
2 teaspoons garlic purée
1 teaspoon dried basil
1 tablespoon dried parsley

freshly ground black pepper
½ teaspoon ground nutmeg
4 oz (100 g) dried wholemeal breadcrumbs
1 teaspoon dried English mustard
3 oz (75 g) strong Cheddar cheese, grated
1 French stick, brown or white

1 Pre-heat the grill. In a saucepan or microwave, defrost the spinach.
2 Cut the pimentoes into strips.
3 Heat the sunflower oil in a large frying pan, add the garlic purée, herbs and black pepper. Lay the tomato slices and pimento strips in the pan, heat through for 1 minute, then remove from heat.

4   Drain the spinach and squeeze out excess water. Season the spinach with nutmeg and black pepper.

5   Spread half the spinach on the bottom of a flameproof dish. Layer over half of the tomato and pimento mixture. Repeat this process once again, finishing with a layer of tomato and pimentoes.

6   In a small bowl, mix together the breadcrumbs, dried mustard and grated cheese.

7   Scatter the cheese mixture over the Florentine layer and place under the hot grill for 4 to 5 minutes until heated through and golden brown.

8   Serve straight away with French bread and the carrot and poppy seed salad.

Variations

1   Cooked broccoli can be used instead of spinach.

2   Any crisp salad goes well with this tasty dish; however, the crunchiness of this carrot and poppy seed salad lends itself best.

▶ CARROT AND POPPY SEED SALAD

4 large carrots, grated	freshly ground black pepper
1 oz (25 g) poppy seeds	½ tablespoon lemon juice

Combine the salad ingredients together well, season to taste with black pepper and pile into a serving dish.

ROOT VEGETABLE COMPOTE WITH MINT AND YOGHURT SAUCE AND PITTA BREAD

This lovely combination of spicy vegetables with cracked wheat makes a delicious complete feast. Marrow, unfortunately, is one of the most under-rated vegetables – give it a try this way.

Serves 4   £££

SHOPPING LIST

2 sticks celery
3 large carrots
1 small swede
1 small marrow
4 wholemeal pitta breads
10 fl oz (300 ml) natural yoghurt

TIME PLAN

1 Follow stages 1 and 2 of compote recipe.
2 Clear decks and prepare yoghurt and mint sauce.
3 Follow stage 3 of compote recipe.
4 Enjoy feast.

▶ **ROOT VEGETABLE COMPOTE**

1 pint (600 ml) vegetable stock
5 fl oz (150 ml) orange juice
1 bay leaf
2 sticks celery, finely chopped
3 large carrots, grated
1 small swede, finely chopped or grated

1 small marrow, peeled and cubed
4 oz (100 g) cracked wheat
2 teaspoons turmeric
½ teaspoon cayenne pepper
freshly ground black pepper
1 tablespoon dill weed
4 wholemeal pitta breads

1 In a very large saucepan or wok covered with a lid, bring the vegetable stock, orange juice and bay leaf to a rapid boil.
2 Add all the remaining ingredients except the dill. Cover and cook over a high heat for 10 minutes.
3 Taste for seasoning, scatter with dill weed and serve straight from the pan with pitta bread and yoghurt sauce.

Variation

Sweet potato may be used instead of swede. Remember, the smaller you cut the vegetables, the quicker they cook.

► MINT AND YOGHURT SAUCE

10 fl oz (300 ml) natural yoghurt   freshly ground black pepper
2 teaspoons mint sauce

Combine the sauce ingredients and taste for seasoning. Serve separately with root vegetable compote.

HIGHLAND FLING FEAST

FRUIT FLUMMERY

A heart-warming stir-fry without a bean sprout in sight!

Serves 4   £££

SHOPPING LIST

4 rashers lean bacon
4 medium-sized potatoes
2 leeks
8 oz (100 g) spring greens
2 Cox's apples
1 × 8-oz (225-g) tin of
    raspberries in natural juice
½ round soda bread
1 pint (600 ml) fromage frais

TIME PLAN

1   Follow stages 1 to 4 of Highland fling feast recipe.
2   Clear decks and prepare fruit flummery; set to one side.
3   Follow stage 5 of Highland fling feast recipe and serve at once with soda bread.

▶ HIGHLAND FLING FEAST

4 medium-sized potatoes, cut
   into thick chips
1 tablespoon sunflower oil
4 rashers lean bacon, diced
2 leeks, washed and cut into large
   slices

2 Cox's apples, cored and sliced
10 fl oz (300 ml) vegetable stock
8 oz (225 g) spring greens,
   washed and shredded
½ round soda bread

1   Par-boil the potatoes for 4 to 5 minutes.
2   In a large frying pan or wok, heat the oil and stir-fry the bacon and leeks for 2 minutes.
3   Drain the potatoes well and add to the bacon and leeks. Stir-fry over a high heat for 2 minutes.
4   Add the sliced apple to the pan, pour in the stock and cook for a further 2 minutes.
5   At the last moment, toss in the shredded spring greens, heat through, and serve straight away with soda bread.

Variation
Leeks are at their best and cheapest in the winter time. However, spring onions make a good alternative.

▶ FRUIT FLUMMERY

1 pint (600 ml) fromage frais
1 × 8-oz (225-g) tin raspberries in
   natural juice, drained and juice
   reserved

4 teaspoons runny honey
4 tablespoons muesli

1   Mix the fromage frais with three-quarters of the raspberries and honey.
2   Divide the raspberry juice into 4 serving glasses.
3   Spoon on half the fromage frais mixture, sprinkle over half the muesli and repeat with a second layer of fromage frais.
4   Sprinkle the remaining muesli on top and decorate with the reserved raspberries.

Variation
An alternative to muesli would be to toast porridge oats under the grill or dry fry them in a saucepan.

CAULIFLOWER RATATOUILLE WITH CRUSTY PAPRIKA ROLLS

PEACH MELT

A simple version of the classic ratatouille that can be made in minutes. The peach melts make a great summer pudding. Tinned peaches or apricot halves can be used when fresh are out of season.

Serves 4   £££

SHOPPING LIST	TIME PLAN
1 medium onion	1 Follow stages 1 and 2 of ratatouille recipe.
1 green pepper	
1 small cucumber	2 Follow stages 1 to 3 of peach melt recipe.
1 small cauliflower	
4 tomatoes	3 Prepare rolls for grilling. Remove peach melt from grill and grill rolls.
4 large fresh peaches or nectarines	
1 × 7-oz (200-g) tin blackcurrants in natural juice	4 Serve ratatouille with crusty rolls.
4 oz (100 g) black olives	
4 large wholemeal rolls	5 Serve peach melt with blackcurrants.
6 oz (175 g) low fat cream cheese	
2 oz (50 g) strong Cheddar cheese	

► CAULIFLOWER RATATOUILLE

1 tablespoon garlic purée
2 teaspoons dried mixed herbs
1 medium onion, grated
1 green pepper
1 cucumber, diced
1 × 14-oz (450-g) carton sieved
  tomatoes
1 bay leaf

1 small cauliflower, broken into
  small florets
1 tablespoon Worcestershire
  sauce
2 tablespoons tomato purée
2 tablespoons dried parsley
4 oz (100 g) black olives, stoned
freshly ground black pepper

58

1   In a saucepan, dry fry the garlic, herbs and grated onion for 30 seconds
2   Add all the remaining ingredients except the olives, cover and simmer rapidly for 8 to 10 minutes.
3   Stir in the olives, season to taste with black pepper. Pile into a dish and serve at once with crusty paprika rolls.

Variations
1   Frozen cauliflower or broccoli can be used in the ratatouille.
2   Ratatouille is just as good served cold and makes a great filling for pancakes or omelettes.

► CRUSTY PAPRIKA ROLLS

4 large wholemeal rolls
1 egg, beaten

2 oz (50 g) strong Cheddar cheese
1 teaspoon paprika

1   Pre-heat the grill.
2   Brush the rolls with the beaten egg.
3   Mix the grated cheese and paprika together and sprinkle over the rolls.
4   Place under the hot grill for 1 minute until melted and golden brown. Serve at once with the cauliflower ratatouille.

► PEACH MELT

The wheat flakes give this pudding a crunchy texture. Nectarines make a good alternative to the peaches.

4 large fresh peaches, halved and stoned
6 oz (175 g) low fat cream cheese
2 oz (50 g) toasted wheat flakes
1 oz (25 g) sesame seeds

few drops vanilla essence
1 oz (25 g) brown sugar
1 × 7-oz (200-g) tin blackcurrants in natural juice

1   Pre-heat the grill.
2   Mix the cream cheese, wheat flakes, sesame seeds and vanilla essence together. Spoon the filling into the peach cavities.
3   Arrange the peaches in a shallow flameproof dish, sprinkle with the brown sugar and place under the grill for 2 to 3 minutes until golden brown and bubbling.
4   Spoon over the blackcurrants and serve at once.

FISH FEASTS

HIGHLAND MACKEREL WITH SESAME SPINACH NOODLES

FRUIT PARCELS

Get your roller skates on for this feast!

Serves 4   £££

SHOPPING LIST

4 large mackerel fillets
3 large tomatoes
1 small bunch fresh parsley
8 large leaves of spinach
3 large ripe pears
1 × 7-oz (200-g) tin blackberries
   in natural juice
10 fl oz (300 ml) fromage frais

TIME PLAN

1   Follow stages 1 to 6 of
    Highland mackerel recipe.
2   Follow stages 1 to 4 of fruit
    parcels recipe.
3   Follow stages 1 to 4 of
    noodles recipe.
4   Serve feast.

► HIGHLAND MACKEREL

4 large mackerel fillets
1 tablespoon French mustard
porridge oats for coating
2 tablespoons sunflower oil
freshly ground black pepper

3 large tomatoes, chopped
2 tablespoons lemon juice
2 tablespoons chopped fresh
   parsley

1   Pre-heat the oven to 400°F (200°C), gas mark 6.
2   Spread the mustard on the skinless side of the mackerel.
3   Roll and coat the mackerel fillets in the oats.
4   Heat the oil in a large frying pan until very hot.
5   Carefully lay in the mackerel fillets, skin side uppermost. Cook for 1 minute or until golden brown. Using a fish slice, turn the mackerel fillets over and cook for a further 1 minute. Lift the mackerel fillets into an ovenproof dish and sprinkle over the chopped tomatoes and lemon juice.
6   Place in the oven for 8 to 10 minutes.
7   Remove the mackerel from the oven, scatter with the parsley and serve.

Variations
1   If you have a flameproof casserole, there is no need to transfer the mackerel fillets after stage 3.
2   Herrings can be used instead of mackerel fillets.

▶ SESAME SPINACH NOODLES

1 × 8-oz (225-g) packet Chinese egg noodles
1 teaspoon sunflower oil
2 tablespoons sesame seeds
4 tablespoons soy sauce

2 teaspoons garlic purée
freshly ground black pepper
8 large leaves of spinach, washed and shredded

1   Plunge the noodles into boiling water and simmer for 3 minutes.
2   Drain the noodles and set to one side.
3   Heat the oil in a large frying pan or wok, add the noodles, sesame seeds, soy sauce and garlic purée. Toss and season with black pepper.
4   Just before serving, add the shredded spinach, toss well and serve at once.

▶ FRUIT PARCELS

1 × 7-oz (200-g) tin blackberries in natural juice
3 large ripe pears, cored and sliced

4 teaspoons honey
1 teaspoon ground ginger
4 tablespoons orange juice
10 fl oz (300 ml) fromage frais

1 Pre-heat the oven to 400°F (200°C), gas mark 6.
2 Cut out 4 large squares of tin foil and place on a baking tray.
3 Divide the fruit equally on to each square of tin foil. Trickle over the honey, ginger and spoon over the orange juice.
4 Close the foil into parcels and bake in the oven for 6 to 8 minutes or until bubbling hot.
5 Serve the fruit in the foil parcels – the diners can open these themselves. Serve with fromage frais.

TUNNY TORTILLA WITH BASIL SAUCE AND COS AND CUCUMBER PLATTER

A quick, colourful omelette with a Spanish theme makes a delicious feast. Follow it with some fresh fruit.

Serves 4   £££

SHOPPING LIST

1 medium onion
1 red pepper
1 small bunch fresh parsley
½ cos lettuce
½ cucumber
fresh fruit of choice for dessert
1 × 6-oz (175-g) tin tuna fish
4 oz (100 g) frozen broad beans
wholemeal bread
4 oz (100 g) cottage cheese

TIME PLAN

1 Follow stages 1 to 4 of tunny tortilla recipe.
2 Combine basil and tomato sauce ingredients and simmer.
3 Clear decks and prepare cos platter.
4 Finish tortilla under the grill.
5 Clear decks and serve feast.

▶ TUNNY TORTILLA

1 tablespoon sunflower oil	freshly ground black pepper
1 medium onion, grated	1 × 6-oz (175-g) tin tuna fish
2 teaspoons garlic purée	1 oz (25 g) dried wholemeal
4 oz (100 g) frozen broad beans	breadcrumbs
1 red pepper, cut into strips	2 tablespoons chopped fresh
4 eggs	parsley
4 oz (100 g) cottage cheese	wholemeal bread

1 Pre-heat the grill.
2 Heat the oil in a large frying pan and add the onion, garlic purée, broad beans and strips of red pepper. Stir-fry for 2 minutes.
3 Meanwhile, in a large mixing bowl, beat together the eggs and cottage cheese and season with black pepper.
4 Flake the tuna fish over the vegetables and pour over the egg mixture, give one quick stir and reduce the heat to medium. Scatter over the breadcrumbs and cook for 3 to 4 minutes until just firm.
5 Finish cooking under the grill until golden brown.
6 To serve, remove the tortilla from the grill, cut into wedges and trickle over some of the basil sauce; serve the rest separately. Scatter over the chopped parsley and serve the tortilla straight from the pan with wholemeal bread and salad.

▶ BASIL SAUCE

1 × 1-lb (450-g) carton sieved	2 teaspoons dried or fresh
tomatoes	chopped basil
2 teaspoons garlic purée	freshly ground black pepper

1 In a saucepan, heat the sauce ingredients together for 6 to 8 minutes.
2 Season to taste with black pepper and serve.

▶ COS AND CUCUMBER PLATTER

See recipe on page 30.

Smoked Haddock Papillotes with Tomato and Thyme Baguette and Green Salad

'Papillote' simply means cooking in a paper bag. This fun way of cooking is easy to do and saves on the washing up. It is also a great surprise for the diners at the table as they unwrap their parcels.

Serves 4   £ £ £ £ £

SHOPPING LIST

1 lb (450 g) smoked haddock
  fillets, skinned
1 bunch spring onions
1 large carrot
1 orange
4 tomatoes
1 round lettuce
1 bunch watercress
1 medium brown French stick

TIME PLAN

1   Follow stages 1 to 3 of haddock papillotes recipe.
2   Complete baguette recipe and place in oven to cook.
3   Wash and prepare salad ingredients and place in serving bowl.
4   Clear decks and prepare orange wedges for fish.
5   Serve feast.

▶ SMOKED HADDOCK PAPILLOTES

1 lb (450 g) smoked haddock
  fillets, skinned and cut into
  strips
10 fl oz (300 ml) orange juice
1 bunch spring onions, chopped

1 large carrot, grated
freshly ground black pepper
4 small bay leaves
1 orange, cut into wedges to
  serve

1   Pre-heat the oven to 425°F (220°C), gas mark 7.
2   Divide the smoked haddock pieces between the 4 pieces of foil. Pour over the orange juice and sprinkle with chopped spring onions and grated carrot. Season with black pepper and place a bay leaf on top.

64

3   Seal each piece of foil to form a parcel. Place the parcels on a baking tray and cook in the oven for 10 minutes.

4   Serve the haddock in the foil parcels, with the orange wedges to garnish.

▶ TOMATO AND THYME BAGUETTE

1 medium brown French stick
sunflower oil for brushing
4 tomatoes, sliced

garlic salt
2 teaspoons dried or fresh
    chopped thyme leaves

1   Pre-heat the oven to 425°F (220°C), gas mark 7.

2   Using a sharp knife, split the French stick in half lengthways. Lightly brush the bread with oil and lay the sliced tomatoes along the bread.

3   Brush the tomato slices lightly with oil and sprinkle over the garlic salt, thyme and freshly ground black pepper.

4   Place both halves on a baking tray and bake in a hot oven for 7 minutes.

▶ GREEN SALAD

1 round lettuce
1 bunch watercress
1 tablespoon lemon juice

2 tablespoons sunflower oil
freshly ground black pepper
garlic salt

Wash and prepare salad ingredients and toss gently in the lemon juice and sunflower oil. Season with black pepper and garlic salt.

Corn Cakes with Salmon and Cucumber Cream

Grilled Bananas with Oats

This is a delicious and interesting way of using tinned salmon. The recipe makes twelve corn cakes.

Serves 4   £££££

SHOPPING LIST

½ cucumber
2 punnets mustard and cress
4 ripe bananas
1 × 6-oz (175-g) tin pink salmon
15 fl oz (450 ml) natural yoghurt
2 oz (50 g) cream cheese

TIME PLAN

1 Pre-heat the grill. Pre-heat the oven to 425°F (220°C), gas mark 7.
2 Follow stages 1 to 6 of corn cakes recipe.
3 Prepare bananas and place under grill.
4 Prepare salmon and cucumber cream and mustard and cress.
5 Clear decks and serve corn cakes with salmon and cucumber cream.
6 Serve bananas when ready.

► CORN CAKES WITH SALMON AND CUCUMBER CREAM

5 oz (150 g) self-raising flour
1 teaspoon bicarbonate of soda
1 tablespoon dill weed
1 teaspoon chilli powder
1 × 7-oz (200-g) tin sweetcorn,
   drained
4 fl oz (100 ml) natural yoghurt
1 egg
1 tablespoon sunflower oil
oil for greasing
paprika for decoration

For the salmon and cucumber
   cream
½ cucumber, grated
1 × 6-oz (175-g) tin pink salmon,
   drained
10 fl oz (300 ml) natural yoghurt
2 oz (50 g) low fat cream cheese
1 teaspoon lemon juice
1 teaspoon dill weed

freshly ground black pepper
2 punnets mustard and cress,
   washed

1   Pre-heat the oven to 425°F (220°C), gas mark 7.
2   Lightly oil a patty tin with 12 indentations.
3   Sift the flour and bicarbonate of soda into a large mixing bowl. Stir in the dill weed, chilli and drained sweetcorn.
4   Make a well in the centre and pour in the yoghurt, egg and oil. Mix briefly.
5   Quickly spoon the mixture into the oiled patty tins, filling them three-quarters full. Do not smooth the surface.
6   Sprinkle the corn cakes with paprika and bake for 10 to 12 minutes.
7   While the corn cakes are cooking, mix all the ingredients together for the salmon and cucumber cream. Season to taste with black pepper.
8   To serve, split the hot corn cakes, place opened on a serving plate (3 cakes per person). Drizzle over the salmon and cucumber cream and scatter with the mustard and cress.

Variation
Try tuna instead of pink salmon.

► GRILLED BANANAS WITH OATS

4 ripe bananas, peeled
5 fl oz (150 ml) orange juice
2 tablespoons brown sugar

1 teaspoon ground cinnamon
2 tablespoons jumbo or porridge
   oats

67

1 Pre-heat the grill.
2 Cut the bananas in half lengthways and lay them in a shallow flameproof dish.
3 Pour over the orange juice and set to one side.
4 In a small bowl, mix the sugar, cinnamon and oats. Scatter over the bananas and place under a medium grill for 6 to 8 minutes. Increase the heat for the final minute to achieve a crisp topping.

Variations
1 Choose very ripe bananas for the pudding as they tend to have more flavour and grill more quickly.
2 Ripe pears make an excellent alternative.

PROVENÇALE COD CASSOULET WITH SODA BREAD

APRICOT AND RASPBERRY SOUP

This tasty feast uses smatana which is made from a mixture of single cream and skimmed milk. It makes a great lower-fat substitute for cream.

Serves 4   £££££

SHOPPING LIST

4 rashers lean bacon
1 lb (450 g) cod fillet
1 round lettuce
2 oz (50 g) Cheddar cheese
½ round soda bread
2 × 14-oz (400-g) tins apricots in natural juice
8 oz (225 g) frozen raspberries
5 fl oz (150 ml) smatana or fromage frais

TIME PLAN

1 Follow stages 1 to 4 of cassoulet recipe.
2 Meanwhile, follow complete soup recipe and pre-heat the grill. Mix together topping for cassoulet.
3 Place cassoulet under grill.
4 Clear decks and serve feast with soda bread.
5 Serve soup.

▶ PROVENÇALE COD CASSOULET

4 rashers lean bacon, diced
1 lb (450 g) cod fillet, skinned
freshly ground black pepper
½ round lettuce
1 × 14-oz (400-g) tin chopped
  tomatoes
1 × 14-oz (400-g) tin flageolet
  beans, drained
1 × 14-oz (400-g) tin butter
  beans, drained

2 teaspoons oregano
garlic salt

For the topping
4 oz (100 g) dried wholemeal
  breadcrumbs
2 oz (50 g) Cheddar cheese,
  grated
2 teaspoons dried oregano
½ round soda bread

1 In a large frying pan, dry fry the bacon pieces. Meanwhile, cut the cod into 4 pieces and season with black pepper.
2 Wrap each piece of fish in lettuce leaves and place on top of bacon.
3 Reduce the heat and pour over the tinned tomatoes and drained beans. Season with black pepper, oregano and garlic salt.
4 Cover the frying pan with a lid or baking tray and simmer for 7 minutes, removing the lid for the last minute.
5 In a small bowl, mix the topping ingredients together and scatter over the beans. Place under the hot grill, turning the pan when necessary to form a lovely golden crust.
6 Serve with chunks of soda bread.

Variation
Plaice, haddock or coley can be used instead of cod.

▶ APRICOT AND RASPBERRY SOUP

2 × 14-oz (400-g) tins apricots in
  natural juice
5 fl oz (150 ml) orange juice
8 oz (225 g) frozen raspberries

4 tablespoons smatana or fromage
  frais
a little milk
2 oz (50 g) flaked almonds,
  toasted

1 Liquidise the apricots and orange juice until smooth. Pour into individual soup bowls and place a heaped tablespoon of the frozen raspberries in the centre of each bowl.
2 Thin the smatana or fromage frais with a little milk and swirl a spoonful onto each soup bowl. Scatter with toasted flaked almonds and serve.

FUN SUPPERS

SAVOURY-LOVERS' SUPPER

For those of you who prefer savoury to sweet, here is the perfect feast.

Serves 4   £££££

SHOPPING LIST

4 large tomatoes
1 punnet mustard and cress
1 lb (450 g) broccoli florets
1 × 14-oz (400-g) tin red
  pimentoes
4 granary rolls
4 oz (100 g) low fat cream cheese
4 slices lean ham

TIME PLAN

1 Steam broccoli.
2 Cook noodles.
3 Follow complete tomato
   recipe.
4 Dry fry sesame seeds, drain
   noodles and follow stages 3
   to 5 of noodle recipe.
5 Finish stage 3 of broccoli
   recipe.
6 Serve feast, take off your
   roller skates!

▶ STUFFED TOMATOES

4 large tomatoes
4 oz (100 g) low fat cream cheese
1 oz (25 g) raisins
1 teaspoon Worcestershire sauce

freshly ground black pepper
1 punnet mustard and cress,
  washed
4 granary rolls

1 Slice a quarter off the top of each tomato.
2 Using a teaspoon, scoop out the flesh and seeds into a small bowl. To
   this add the cream cheese, raisins, Worcestershire sauce and black
   pepper. Mix together.

3   Fill the hollowed-out tomatoes with the cream cheese mixture and place the tomato lids on top.
4   Place on a serving plate and scatter with mustard and cress.
5   Serve with granary rolls.

▶ NOODLES CARBONARA

8 oz (225 g) Chinese egg noodles
1 tablespoon sunflower oil
1 × 14-oz (400-g) tin red
    pimentoes, drained and cut
    into strips

4 slices lean ham, cut into strips
garlic salt
freshly ground black pepper

1   To cook the noodles, plunge them into boiling water and simmer for 3 minutes.
2   Drain the noodles.
3   Heat the sunflower oil in a large frying pan or wok.
4   Add the pimentoes, ham strips and garlic salt and stir-fry for 1 minute.
5   Add the noodles and toss well until heated through.
6   Season with black pepper and serve immediately.

▶ STEAMED SESAME BROCCOLI

1 lb (450 g) broccoli florets
1 oz (25 g) sesame seeds

1 tablespoon lemon juice
freshly ground black pepper

1   Place the washed broccoli in a steamer or metal sieve. Set the steamer in a saucepan and pour in enough water to come a third of the way up the saucepan. (The vegetables should not be sitting in the water.) Cover the saucepan with a tight-fitting lid (to trap steam). Steam the vegetables for 8 to 10 minutes or until tender.
2   Dry fry the sesame seeds in a small saucepan until lightly toasted, approximately 30 seconds.
3   Remove the broccoli from steamer and place it in a serving dish. Sprinkle with lemon juice and scatter over the sesame seeds and black pepper.

AVOCADO GRATIN WITH SPINACH SUPREME

SPICED MELON

Serves 4 £ £ £ £ £

SHOPPING LIST

2 large ripe avocadoes
1 lemon
6 spring onions
8 oz (225 g) spinach
1 punnet cherry tomatoes or
  6 small tomatoes
4 oz (100 g) button mushrooms
2 small melons
2 × 4-oz (100-g) tins smoked
  mussels
granary bread
2 oz (50 g) low fat cream cheese
  or quark
5 fl oz (150 ml) fromage frais
10 fl oz (300 ml) Greek yoghurt
2 oz (50 g) Cheddar cheese

TIME PLAN

1   Follow stages 1 and 2 of
    spiced melon recipe.
2   Pre-heat the grill.
3   Prepare spinach.
4   Follow stages 1 to 5 of
    avocado recipe.
5   Make salad dressing, put salad
    together.
6   Serve feast.

► AVOCADO GRATIN

2 × 4-oz (100-g) tins smoked
  mussels, drained
2 oz (50 g) low fat cream cheese
  or quark
5 fl oz (150 ml) fromage frais
6 spring onions, chopped
1 teaspoon garlic purée
2 teaspoons lemon juice
freshly ground black pepper

2 large ripe avocadoes

For the topping
2 tablespoons dried wholemeal
  breadcrumbs
1 oz (25 g) Cheddar cheese, grated

1 lemon cut into wedges for
  garnish
granary bread

1   Pre-heat the grill.
2   Mix the mussels with the cream cheese and carefully mix in the fromage frais. Then add the spring onions, garlic purée and lemon juice and season to taste with black pepper.
3   Cut the avocadoes in half lengthways and remove the stones.
4   Spoon the mussel mixture over the avocado halves and sprinkle with the crumb and cheese topping.
5   Place under the hot grill for 2 to 3 minutes until bubbling and golden.
6   Serve straight away, garnished with the lemon wedges and served with chunks of granary bread.

▶ **SPINACH SUPREME**

8 oz (225 g) spinach
1 punnet cherry tomatoes or
    6 small tomatoes, quartered
4 oz (100 g) button mushrooms,
    halved

For the dressing
3 tablespoons sunflower oil
1 tablespoon orange juice
2 teaspoons runny honey
1 teaspoon wholegrain mustard
freshly ground black pepper

1   Pick over the spinach leaves and wash well, then tear into bite-size pieces and combine with the tomatoes and mushrooms.
2   In a small bowl, beat the dressing ingredients together and season to taste with black pepper.
3   Pour the dressing over the salad ingredients and toss well.
4   Serve with the avocado gratin.

▶ **SPICED MELON**

10 fl oz (300 ml) Greek yoghurt
1 teaspoon ground ginger
1 teaspoon mixed spice

2 small melons, halved and
    deseeded
1 tablespoon brown sugar

1   Mix the Greek yoghurt with the spices.
2   Spoon into the melon hollows, sprinkle with brown sugar and place in refrigerator.
3   Serve well chilled.

TANDOORI TIÈDE SALAD WITH CRUSTY ROLLS

APRICOT AND GINGER CREAM

An unusual and interesting 'salad tiède' – which simply means a warm salad. Make sure all the delicious juices from the pan are drizzled over the salad leaves. This feast is followed by a refreshing apricot and ginger cream which will really cleanse your palate.

Serves 4   £££££

SHOPPING LIST

12 oz (350 g) skinned, boneless chicken flesh
1 cos lettuce
½ cucumber
1 bunch watercress
8 oz (225 g) bean sprouts
1 × 14-oz (400-g) tin apricots in natural juice
4 crusty wholemeal rolls
1 pint (600 ml) fromage frais

TIME PLAN

1   Make apricot and ginger cream and leave in refrigerator to chill.
2   Clear decks.
3   Follow complete salad recipe.
4   Serve feast.

▶ **TANDOORI TIÈDE SALAD**

12 oz (350 g) skinned, boneless chicken flesh, cut into finger-like strips
3 tablespoons tandoori or tikka paste
1 tablespoon lemon juice
1 teaspoon garlic purée
1 tablespoon sunflower oil
1 cos lettuce, washed and torn into bite-size pieces

½ cucumber, chopped into bite-size pieces
1 bunch watercress, washed and picked over
8 oz (225 g) bean sprouts
freshly ground black pepper
4 crusty wholemeal rolls

1   Toss the chicken strips with the tandoori paste, lemon juice and garlic purée.
2   Heat the oil in a large frying pan or wok.
3   Add the coated chicken and any extra sauce and stir-fry for about 3 to 4 minutes over a high heat until cooked, reducing the heat if necessary.
4   Meanwhile, wash and prepare the salad ingredients and divide between 4 large plates.
5   Add the bean sprouts to the chicken, season with black pepper and stir-fry for a further 2 minutes.
6   Spoon the chicken, bean sprouts and juices over the salad and serve immediately with crusty wholemeal rolls.

Variation
The salad can be made completely vegetarian by using vegetables tossed in tandoori paste instead of chicken.

▶ **APRICOT AND GINGER CREAM**

1 × 14-oz (400-g) tin apricots in natural juice, drained
2 teaspoons ground ginger

1 pint (600 ml) fromage frais
4 teaspoons honey

1   With a fork, roughly mash the apricots and ground ginger.
2   Spoon the fromage frais into a mixing bowl.
3   With a large spoon carefully fold the apricot mix into the fromage frais.
4   Spoon into 4 wine glasses and drizzle over the honey.
5   Place in refrigerator to chill.

Variation
Peaches can be used instead of apricots.

SURPRISE PASTA BREAD

RASPBERRY CHEESE WITH STRAWBERRY CRUDITÉS

This fun supper is best served in the summertime when strawberries are at their best and cheapest.

Serves 4   £££££

SHOPPING LIST

1 lb (450 g) strawberries
4 oz (100 g) mushrooms
1 × 4-oz (100-g) tin smoked
  mussels or tuna fish
1 × 7-oz (200-g) tin raspberries in
  natural juice
4 oz (100 g) low fat cream cheese
1 large round cottage loaf or
  granary cob

TIME PLAN

1 Follow stages 1 to 4 of
   surprise pasta bread recipe.
2 Prepare and assemble
   strawberry pudding.
3 Finish off surprise pasta bread
   and serve feast.
4 Serve dessert when ready.

► SURPRISE PASTA BREAD

12 oz (350 g) wholewheat small
  pasta shells
1 × 1¼-lb (500-g) carton sieved
  tomatoes
4 oz (100 g) mushrooms, sliced
2 teaspoons garlic purée
1 teaspoon dried thyme

2 tablespoons Worcestershire
  sauce
1 large round cottage loaf or
  granary cob
1 × 4-oz (100-g) tin smoked
  mussels or tuna fish, drained
freshly ground black pepper

1   Pre-heat the oven to 400°F (200°C), gas mark 6.
2   Cook the pasta in boiling water for 8 to 10 minutes.
3   In a saucepan, mix together the sieved tomatoes, sliced mushrooms, garlic purée, thyme and Worcestershire sauce, and simmer for 5 minutes.
4   Cut the top off the cottage loaf and hollow out the bread. Place the hollowed bread and lid into the oven.
5   Drain the pasta, then return it to the saucepan and add the mussels and black pepper; toss gently.
6   Check the tomato sauce for seasoning and pour over the pasta.
7   Remove the bread from the oven, fill with the pasta and top with the lid.
8   Serve extra pasta separately.

Note

When hollowing out your loaf don't throw away the bread from the centre; this can be used for breadcrumbs, thickening soups, stews and even making toasted croûtons for soups or salads.

▶ RASPBERRY CHEESE WITH STRAWBERRY CRUDITÉS

1 lb (450 g) strawberries
1 × 7-oz (200-g) tin raspberries in natural juice, drained and juice reserved

2 tablespoons raspberry juice
4 oz (100 g) low fat cream cheese

1   Wash the strawberries and arrange them on a large plate.
2   In a small mixing bowl, beat together the drained raspberries with 2 tablespoons of juice and the cream cheese.
3   Spoon the cheese into a serving bowl and place on a large plate with the strawberries ready for dipping.

GREEK MEZE

Meze means a selection of tasty dishes. Serve fresh bread or pitta bread with your meze to mop up the juices in a typical Greek way.

Serves 4   £££££

SHOPPING LIST

2 lemons
½ cucumber
1 green pepper
1 medium onion
6 tomatoes
fruit of choice for platter
4 × 4½-oz (125-g) tins sardines in tomato sauce
8 black olives, stoned
1 packet wholemeal pitta bread
10 fl oz (300 ml) natural thick set yoghurt

TIME PLAN

1 Prepare stages 1 to 4 of Mediterranean sardines recipe and place to one side.
2 Prepare Greek salad.
3 Prepare tzatziki and grill pitta bread.
4 Follow stage 5 of Mediterranean sardines recipe.
5 Prepare Greek fruit platter.
6 Remove sardines from grill and serve feast.

► TZATZIKI

10 fl oz (300 ml) natural thick set yoghurt
2 teaspoons garlic purée
½ cucumber, washed and grated

1 teaspoon mint sauce
freshly ground black pepper
1 packet wholemeal pitta bread

1 Mix yoghurt, garlic purée, cucumber and mint sauce together and season to taste with black pepper, then spoon into a serving dish.
2 Toast the pitta bread and cut it into thick strips.

▶ MEDITERRANEAN SARDINES

2 × 4½-oz (125-g) tin sardines in tomato sauce
zest and juice of 1 lemon

1 teaspoon dried mixed herbs
freshly ground black pepper

1 Pre-heat the grill.
2 Carefully lay the sardines with the tomato sauce in a large shallow flameproof dish.
3 Grate over the lemon zest and squeeze over the lemon juice.
4 Scatter with the mixed herbs and grind over plenty of black pepper.
5 Place the sardines under the grill and cook for 4 to 5 minutes.
6 Serve straight away.

Variation
Pilchards or sardines in oil can also be used for this dish.

▶ GREEK-STYLE SALAD

6 tomatoes, cut into large chunks
1 green pepper, thinly sliced
1 medium onion, thinly sliced
8 black olives, stoned
1 × 14-oz (400-g) tin chick peas, drained

1 teaspoon dried oregano
1 tablespoon lemon juice
1 tablespoon sunflower oil
freshly ground black pepper

1 Mix all the salad ingredients and chick peas in a large bowl. Add the oregano, lemon juice, sunflower oil and black pepper.
2 Gently toss the salad together and serve.

▶ QUICK GREEK-STYLE FRUIT PLATTER

a selection of fresh seasonal fruits, such as bananas, pears, apples, peaches, oranges

crushed ice
juice of ½ lemon

1 Wash and prepare the fruits.
2 Cut or segment the fruit into large bite-size pieces.
3 Crunch the ice to cover the bottom of a large plate.
4 Arrange the fruit over the ice, sprinkle with lemon juice and more crushed ice.
5 Leave to chill for 5 minutes and serve.

CHEESE AND APPLE FONDUE

PINEAPPLE SURPRISE

Fondues are easy to prepare and great fun to eat. Don't despair if you don't have a fondue set, you can easily set up your own. You need a medium-size saucepan to make the fondue sauce, forks for dipping and a roasting tray with four night lights with a wire cooling rack over the top to keep your fondue sauce warm at the table.

Serves 4   £££££

SHOPPING LIST

2 red apples
2 ripe William pears
1 large ripe pineapple
1 cucumber
1 bunch radishes
1 small bunch fresh parsley
1 brown French stick
5 fl oz (150 ml) apple juice
4 thin slices lean ham
4 oz (100 g) Emmenthal or Edam cheese
10 fl oz (300 ml) fromage frais

TIME PLAN

1   Follow complete pineapple surprise recipe on page 82 and set to one side.
2   Follow stages 1 to 3 of fondue recipe.
3   Follow complete fondue dip bits recipe.
4   Finish fondue recipe.
5   Serve feast.

▶ CHEESE AND APPLE FONDUE

1 pint (600 ml) vegetable stock
1 heaped teaspoon garlic purée
2 red apples, cored and diced
5 fl oz (150 ml) apple juice
2 tablespoons lemon juice
3 teaspoons cornflour

4 oz (100 g) Emmenthal or Edam cheese, grated
3 teaspoons French mustard
1 small bunch fresh parsley, chopped
freshly ground black pepper

1   In a medium-size saucepan, mix together the vegetable stock, garlic purée and diced apples.
2   Cover and bring to a rapid boil until the liquid has reduced by half (this should take about 5 minutes).
3   In a small bowl, mix the apple juice, lemon juice and cornflour.
4   Remove the saucepan from the heat and pour in the cornflour mixture. Return the saucepan to the heat and bring slowly to the boil, stirring continuously (it will go alarmingly lumpy but just carry on whisking until the sauce is smooth). Bring to the boil and simmer for 30 seconds. Stir in the grated cheese, mustard, chopped parsley and black pepper.
5   Keep fondue warm until ready to serve.

► FONDUE DIP BITS

1 brown French stick, cut into bite-size pieces
2 ripe William pears
4 thin slices lean ham

1 cucumber, cut into large bite-size chunks
1 bunch radishes, topped and tailed

1   Pre-heat the oven to 350°F (180°C), gas mark 4.
2   Place the bread chunks in a roasting tin and put in the oven to toast for 5 minutes.
3   Cut the pears in half, then into quarters, and remove the cores. Cut into large chunks.
4   Cut the ham into large strips and wrap it around the pear chunks. Arrange on a large platter with the cucumber chunks and radishes.
5   Remove the bread from the oven and pile into a basket or serving dish.
6   To serve the fondue feast: place the vegetable and ham platter on the table with the basket of warm bread. Take your fondue pot to the table and place on wire rack over night lights.
7   Make sure each guest is armed with a fork and napkin.

▶ PINEAPPLE SURPRISE

1 large ripe pineapple   10 fl oz (300 ml) fromage frais

1   Cut the top and bottom off the pineapple.
2   Set the leafy top to one side.
3   With a small sharp knife, cut around the inside of the skin, working at one end at a time.
4   Carefully push to release the pineapple from its skin.
5   Stand the pineapple skin in a shallow bowl and set to one side.
6   Cut the tube of pineapple flesh into 1-inch (2-cm) slices.
7   Pop the pineapple slices back into the pineapple skin.
8   Replace the leafy top and serve with fromage frais.

USE YOUR LOAF – IDEAS FOR SOME TASTY FEASTS!

PEAR AND POPPY SEED BAGNA

GRAPE AND LOGANBERRY POTS

The combination of pears and blue cheese topped with poppy seeds is mouth-watering. However, if blue cheese is not to your taste use Cheddar or Edam cheese instead.

Serves 4   £££

SHOPPING LIST

4 tomatoes
3 ripe pears
1 round or Webb's lettuce
6 oz (175 g) grapes
1 × 7-oz (200-g) tin loganberries
   in natural juice
4 wholemeal baps
15 fl oz (450 ml) fromage frais
4 oz (100 g) blue cheese
4 slices lean ham

TIME PLAN

1   Pre-heat the grill.
2   Follow stages 1 and 2 of fruit
    pots recipe (overleaf).
3   Brown flaked almonds under
    grill and set to one side.
4   Follow stages 2 to 5 of pear
    and poppy seed bagna recipe
    (overleaf).
5   Clear decks and prepare
    lettuce.
6   Sprinkle almonds and
    cinnamon over pots.
7   Remove bagna, sprinkle with
    poppy seeds and serve feast.

▶ PEAR AND POPPY SEED BAGNA

4 wholemeal baps
4 tomatoes, thinly sliced
1 teaspoon garlic purée
freshly ground black pepper
4 slices lean ham, cut into strips
4 tablespoons fromage frais
1 teaspoon French mustard

3 ripe pears, cored and thinly
  sliced
4 oz (100 g) blue cheese, grated
  or crumbled
1 tablespoon poppy seeds
1 round or Webb's lettuce,
  washed

1 Pre-heat the grill.
2 Split and toast the baps.
3 Arrange the tomato slices over the baps and season with garlic purée and black pepper.
4 In a small mixing bowl, combine the ham, fromage frais and mustard. Spread over the tomatoes and lay the pear slices on top.
5 Sprinkle the baps with cheese and place under the hot grill for 3 to 4 minutes (reducing the heat if necessary) until golden.
6 Remove from the grill, sprinkle with poppy seeds and serve garnished with salad leaves.

▶ GRAPE AND LOGANBERRY POTS

6 oz (175 g) grapes, halved and
  deseeded
1 × 7-oz (200-g) tin loganberries
  in natural juice

10 fl oz (300 ml) fromage frais
4 oz (100 g) flaked almonds
1 teaspoon ground cinnamon

1 Divide the grapes between 4 ramekins or teacups. Spoon over the loganberries and juice.
2 Cover the fruit with the fromage frais and smooth over the surface. Chill in the freezer for 8 minutes.
3 Brown the flaked almonds under the grill (watch them carefully).
4 To serve: sprinkle the pots with the toasted almonds and cinnamon.

SAVOURY BREAD PUDDING WITH TOMATO AND THYME SAUCE AND SALAD WITH RAISIN DRESSING

Here's a savoury version of the famous bread and butter pudding. To enable this dish to cook in time you will need a large shallow ovenproof dish – a quiche or tart dish would be ideal. Follow the feast with a choice of fresh fruit.

Serves 4   £££

SHOPPING LIST

1 bunch spring onions
1 round or Webb's lettuce
3 large carrots
1 bunch watercress
fresh fruit of choice for dessert
1 × 6-oz (175-g) tin pink salmon
5 slices granary bread
2 oz (50 g) Cheddar cheese
5 fl oz (150 ml) fromage frais

TIME PLAN

1   Follow stages 1 to 8 of savoury bread pudding recipe.
2   Clear decks and follow complete salad recipe.
3   Wash and prepare fruit for dessert.
4   Set table and serve feast.

► SAVOURY BREAD PUDDING

5 slices granary bread
low fat spread
1 × 6-oz (175-g) tin pink salmon, drained and juice reserved
1 bunch spring onions, chopped
2 large eggs
8 fl oz (250 ml) skimmed milk
½ teaspoon ground nutmeg
freshly ground black pepper
2 oz (50 g) Cheddar cheese, grated

For the sauce
1 × 1¼-lb (500-g) carton sieved tomatoes
1 teaspoon garlic purée
2 teaspoons dried thyme
1 tablespoon Worcestershire sauce
freshly ground black pepper

85

1   Pre-heat the oven to 425°F (220°C), gas mark 7.
2   Butter the bread and cut each slice into 4 triangles.
3   Place the bread in a large shallow flameproof dish and flake over the salmon.
4   In a mixing bowl, beat together the chopped spring onions, eggs, milk, salmon juice and nutmeg, and season with black pepper.
5   Pour over the bread and salmon.
6   Scatter over the grated cheese and grind over some black pepper.
7   Bake in the oven for 8 minutes.
8   Meanwhile, pre-heat the grill and, in a saucepan, simmer the sauce ingredients together for 4 to 5 minutes.
9   Finish the savoury bread pudding under the hot grill for 1 to 2 minutes until brown and puffed up. Hand the tomato and thyme sauce separately.

▶ SALAD WITH RAISIN DRESSING

1 round or Webb's lettuce
1 bunch watercress, washed and
    picked over
3 large carrots, grated

For the dressing
2 tablespoons orange juice
1 tablespoon lemon juice
5 fl oz (150 ml) fromage frais
1 teaspoon French mustard
4 oz (100 g) raisins
freshly ground black pepper

1   Wash and prepare the lettuce, watercress and carrots. Place in a large salad or serving bowl.
2   In a small bowl, beat together the dressing ingredients. Season to taste with black pepper.
3   Drizzle the dressing over the salad and serve.

QUICK CHILLI PIE WITH RELISH COOLERS

Ideal for lunch or supper, make this chilli pie as hot and spicy as you wish – the coolers are there to come to your rescue. You can use any left-over cheese you may have, but I love it with Stilton. Fresh fruit makes a tasty dessert.

Serves 4   £££

SHOPPING LIST

¼ cucumber
3 carrots
fresh fruit of choice for dessert
1 small brown French stick
2 oz (50 g) Stilton cheese or other blue cheese
5 fl oz (150 ml) natural yoghurt
6 oz (175 g) salami or ham

TIME PLAN

1 Follow stages 1 and 2 of chilli pie recipe.
2 Prepare carrot and cucumber coolers (overleaf).
3 Clear decks and prepare fresh fruit for dessert.
4 Follow stages 3 to 5 of chilli pie recipe.
5 Set table and serve feast.

▶ QUICK CHILLI PIE

1 × 14-oz (400-g) tin butter beans, drained
1 × 14-oz (400-g) tin beans in tomato sauce
1 × 14-oz (400-g) tin kidney beans, drained
1 × 1¼-lb (500-g) carton sieved tomatoes
6 oz (175 g) salami or ham, chopped
2 tablespoons Worcestershire sauce

1½ teaspoons chilli powder
2 teaspoons garlic purée
freshly ground black pepper

For the topping
2 tablespoons wholegrain mustard
1 tablespoon sunflower oil
2 oz (50 g) Stilton cheese, grated

1 small brown French stick

1   Pre-heat the grill.
2   In a saucepan, simmer together all the chilli ingredients for 8 to 10 minutes.
3   Mix the mustard, sunflower oil and Stilton together. Spread the bread with the mustard butter and set to one side.
4   Taste and season the chilli and pour into a shallow flameproof dish. Arrange the bread slices, mustard side up, and push gently down on to the beans.
5   Place under the hot grill for 3 to 4 minutes until the topping is golden brown. Serve with the relish coolers.

▶ **RELISH COOLERS**

For cucumber cooler
5 fl oz (150 ml) natural yoghurt
¼ cucumber, grated
freshly ground black pepper

For carrot cooler
3 carrots, grated
1 tablespoon lemon juice
1 teaspoon honey
freshly ground black pepper

Mix together the cooler ingredients and spoon into separate bowls to serve.

Sardine Muffin Melts

Stir-Fry Fruit

This is really just a fancy version of sardines on toast. However, it looks and tastes far more delicious and you can prepare and cook this dish in minutes. The dessert for your feast is a stir-fry of fruit with exotic flavourings.

Serves 4   £££

SHOPPING LIST

4 oz (100 g) small mushrooms
4 tomatoes
½ cucumber
1 ripe banana
½ iceberg lettuce or curly endive
fresh mint leaves
3 × 4½-oz (120-g) tins sardines in
    tomato sauce
1 × 14-oz (400-g) tin lychees
5 fl oz (150 ml) exotic fruit juice
8 muesli-type biscuits
4 wholemeal muffins
3 oz (75 g) strong Cheddar
    cheese

TIME PLAN

1   Pre-heat the grill.
2   Follow stages 1 to 3 of
    sardine melts recipe.
3   Complete stage 1 of stir-fry
    fruit recipe (overleaf).
4   Grill sardine melts.
5   Prepare salad and clear decks.
6   Add lychees to stir-fry fruit
    and set to one side.
7   Serve feast.

► SARDINE MUFFIN MELTS

3 × 4½-oz (120-g) tins sardines in
    tomato sauce
1 teaspoon garlic purée
3 oz (75 g) strong Cheddar
    cheese, grated
4 oz (100 g) small mushrooms,
    sliced

4 wholemeal muffins
4 tomatoes, thinly sliced
2 teaspoons dried thyme
freshly ground black pepper
½ iceberg lettuce or curly endive,
    torn into bite-size pieces
½ cucumber, sliced

1 Pre-heat the grill.
2 Mash the sardines and mix with the garlic purée, cheese and mush-rooms.
3 Toast the muffins on both sides, then split them in half and spread each half with the sardine mixture. Arrange the tomato slices on top and sprinkle with thyme.
4 Grind over plenty of black pepper and grill for 4 to 5 minutes until bubbling hot.
5 Take 4 large plates and place 2 muffin melts on each, surround with plenty of salad leaves and cucumber. Serve at once.

▶ STIR-FRY FRUIT

1 × 14-oz (400-g) tin lychees,
 drained and juice reserved
5 fl oz (150 ml) exotic fruit juice
8 oz (225 g) dried apricots
1 teaspoon ground ginger

1 bay leaf
1 ripe banana, sliced
fresh mint leaves to garnish
8 muesli-type biscuits

1 In a wok or frying pan, pour in the lychee and exotic juice. Add the dried apricots and spices. Cover and bring to the boil, then remove the lid and simmer for 5 minutes.
2 Add the drained lychees and sliced banana, scatter over the mint leaves and serve hot, warm or cold with muesli biscuits.

BREKKY FEASTS

Don't skip breakfast. You should always try to make time for this important meal. Forget the stodgy British fry-up that finishes you off before you've even begun the day. Here are some breakfasts that will stoke up your body and give you plenty of energy for the day ahead. You don't have to save these recipes just for breakfast – they're great to eat at any time!

BREAKFAST PEP-UP

BANANA BRUNCH

Serves 4   £££

SHOPPING LIST

4 small ripe bananas
2 large ripe pears
4 tablespoons crunchy breakfast
 cereal
1 × 11-oz (300-g) tin loganberries
 or raspberries in natural juice
4 slices thick wholemeal bread or
 4 muffins
1 pint (600 ml) natural or
 flavoured yoghurt

TIME PLAN

1 Pre-heat the grill.
2 Prepare banana brunch and
   place under grill.
3 Prepare and serve breakfast
   pep-up.
4 Remove banana brunch from
   grill and serve straight away.

► BREAKFAST PEP-UP

1 pint (600 ml) natural or
  flavoured yoghurt
2 large ripe pears, cored and
  sliced
4 oz (100 g) sultanas or chopped
  dried figs

2 oz (50 g) hazelnuts, chopped
4 tablespoons crunchy breakfast
  cereal
1 × 11-oz (300-g) tin loganberries
  or raspberries in natural juice

1 Spoon the yoghurt into 4 breakfast bowls.
2 Scatter over the pear slices, sultanas or figs and chopped hazelnuts.
3 Sprinkle over the breakfast cereal and top with the loganberries and
   juice.

► BANANA BRUNCH

4 thick slices wholemeal bread or
  muffins, toasted
runny honey

4 small ripe bananas
pinch of cinnamon
sunflower seeds

1 Spread the toasted bread with a little honey.
2 Mash the banana with a pinch of cinnamon, spread on to the bread
   and sprinkle over a little more cinnamon. Place under the grill until
   bubbling hot. Scatter with sunflower seeds and serve cut into thick
   wedges.

HIGHLAND APRICOTS WITH CARROT AND SESAME BUTTIES AND ST CLEMENT'S TODDY

Serves 4   £££

SHOPPING LIST

2 lemons
4 oranges
3 large carrots
¼ cucumber
8 slices granary or wholemeal
  bread
10 fl oz (300 ml) fromage frais

TIME PLAN

1 Follow stage 1 of Highland apricots recipe.
2 Follow stage 1 of St Clement's toddy recipe (overleaf) and leave to simmer.
3 Follow complete butties recipe (overleaf).
4 Continue stages 2 and 3 of Highland apricots recipe.
5 Finish toddy recipe.
6 Finish stage 4 of butties recipe.
7 Serve brekky feast.

▶ HIGHLAND APRICOTS

6 oz (175 g) dried apricots
6 oz (175 g) prunes, stoned
3 tablespoons porridge oats

2 oz (50 g) hazelnuts, chopped
2 oranges, peeled and sliced
10 fl oz (300 ml) fromage frais

1 In a saucepan, cover the apricots and prunes with water. Simmer uncovered for approximately 10 minutes. Allow to cool slightly.
2 Meanwhile, toast the oats and nuts under the grill, taking care not to over-colour.
3 Mix the oranges with the cooked fruit and divide into 4 breakfast bowls. Spoon over the fromage frais and scatter over the toasted porridge oats and hazelnuts.

▶ CARROT AND SESAME BUTTIES

2 tablespoons sesame seeds,
  toasted
2 tablespoons crunchy peanut
  butter
2 teaspoons soy sauce

3 large carrots, washed and grated
¼ cucumber, grated
freshly ground black pepper
8 slices granary or wholemeal
  bread

1 Pre-heat the grill.
2 In a bowl, mix together the sesame seeds, peanut butter and soy sauce.
3 Add the grated carrot and cucumber and season to taste with black
   pepper.
4 Toast the bread lightly on both sides and sandwich together with the
   filling. Cut each butty into 4 and serve straight away.

▶ ST CLEMENT'S TODDY

1 teaspoon ground nutmeg
1 teaspoon ground ginger
1 bay leaf
1¼ pints (750 ml) water

juice of 2 lemons
juice of 2 oranges
1 teaspoon ground cinnamon

1 Add the nutmeg, ginger and bay leaf to the water and bring to the boil
   in a saucepan. Simmer gently for 5 minutes.
2 Pour the boiling, spiced water on to the orange and lemon juice and
   sprinkle over the ground cinnamon.

BREAKFAST SCONES WITH COTTAGE CHEESE

GRILLED ORANGES WITH NUTMEG AND MAPLE REFRESHER

These scones actually take 12 minutes to cook, but take no time to mix. You can serve them straight from the oven. So get your roller skates on!

Serves 4   £££

SHOPPING LIST

2 punnets mustard and cress
4 oranges
15 fl oz (450 ml) natural yoghurt
8 oz (225 g) low fat cottage
  cheese

TIME PLAN

1   Follow stages 1 to 4 of breakfast scones recipe. Pre-heat the grill.
2   Prepare nutmeg and maple refresher and oranges for grilling.
3   Place oranges under hot grill.
4   Clear decks and serve warm scones with cottage cheese and mustard and cress.
5   Serve oranges with nutmeg and maple refresher.

▶ BREAKFAST SCONES

2 oz (50 g) sunflower margarine
8 oz (225 g) self-raising flour
3 to 4 tablespoons semi-skimmed
  milk
2 oz (50 g) raisins
milk for glazing
1 teaspoon poppy seeds

For the filling
8 oz (225 g) low fat cottage
  cheese
2 punnets mustard and cress,
  washed

95

1   Pre-heat the oven to 425°F (220°C), gas mark 7.
2   Using your fingertips, rub the sunflower margarine into the flour until the mixture resembles coarse breadcrumbs. Stir in the milk and raisins and mix quickly to form a soft not sticky dough, adding extra milk if necessary.
3   Turn the scone dough out on to a floured surface and knead briefly. Roll and pat out to a thickness of ¾ inch (2 cm) and, using a 2-inch (5-cm) cutter, cut into rounds.
4   Place on a floured baking tray, lightly brush with milk and sprinkle with poppy seeds. Bake for 10 to 12 minutes.
5   Serve split in half and filled with cottage cheese and mustard and cress.

▶ GRILLED ORANGES

4 oranges   honey or brown sugar

1   Pre-heat the grill.
2   Cut the oranges in half. Sprinkle with the honey or brown sugar and place under the hot grill for 3 to 4 minutes until bubbling hot. Serve straight away.

▶ NUTMEG AND MAPLE REFRESHER

15 fl oz (450 ml) natural yoghurt   1 teaspoon ground nutmeg
5 fl oz (150 ml) semi-skimmed   4 teaspoons maple syrup or runny
  milk   honey

1   Place all the ingredients in a bowl and mix well.
2   Pour into glasses and sprinkle with extra nutmeg to serve.

TINY TOTS' FEASTS

EGGY BREAD AND VEGETABLE STICKS

FRUITY PORRIDGE

Tempt your toddler with these quick and easy feasts.

Serves 4   £

SHOPPING LIST

½ cucumber
2 large carrots
1 red apple
1 × 7-oz (200-g) tin peaches in
  natural juice
4 slices granary or wholemeal
  bread

TIME PLAN

1 Follow stages 1 to 4 of
   porridge recipe and set to
   one side.
2 Follow stages 1 to 3 of eggy
   bread recipe.
3 Clear decks and serve feast.

▶ **EGGY BREAD WITH VEGETABLE STICKS**

2 large eggs
3 tablespoons milk
4 slices granary or wholemeal
  bread
1 tablespoon sunflower oil

For the vegetable sticks
½ cucumber, sliced
2 large carrots, peeled and cut
  into sticks
1 red apple, cored and cut into
  wedges

1 In a large mixing bowl, beat the eggs and milk together.
2 Dip the bread into the egg mixture and fry quickly on both sides in the sunflower oil.
3 Cut into triangles or fingers and serve straight away with the vegetable sticks.

▶ FRUITY PORRIDGE

1 cup porridge oats
15 fl oz (450 ml) milk

1×7-oz (200-g) tin peaches in natural juice

1 Put the oats and milk into a saucepan and bring to the boil, stirring continuously. Reduce the heat and simmer for 2 to 3 minutes.
2 Liquidise or mash the peaches in their juice.
3 When the porridge is thick and creamy, stir in half the peach purée and spoon into 4 breakfast bowls.
4 Drizzle over the remaining peach purée and serve.

FISHY FEASTS

FRUITY YOGHURT

Serves 4   £££

SHOPPING LIST

2 carrots
2 punnets mustard and cress
6 oz (150 g) fresh fruit of choice
1×6-oz (175-g) tin pink salmon
4 slices wholemeal bread
5 fl oz (150 ml) fromage frais
10 fl oz (300 ml) natural yoghurt

TIME PLAN

1 Hard boil eggs.
2 Prepare fruit yoghurt and set to one side.
3 Prepare fishy feasts.
4 Serve tiny tots' feast.

▶ FISHY FEASTS

1 × 6-oz (175-g) tin pink salmon, drained and flaked
2 teaspoons lemon juice
5 fl oz (150 ml) fromage frais
2 teaspoons tomato ketchup
1 × 7-oz (200-g) tin sweetcorn, drained
2 carrots, grated
2 punnets mustard and cress, washed
2 hard-boiled eggs
4 slices wholemeal bread
sunflower margarine or butter for spreading

1 In a mixing bowl, combine the salmon, lemon juice, fromage frais, tomato ketchup and sweetcorn.
2 Pile this mixture equally in the centre of 4 plates.
3 Mix the grated carrot and mustard and cress together, and arrange around the fish.
4 Finely chop the hard-boiled eggs and scatter over the fish plates.
5 Serve with wholemeal bread and butter.

▶ FRUITY YOGHURT

6 oz (150 g) fresh fruit, chopped
10 fl oz (300 ml) natural yoghurt
honey to taste

1 Mix together the fresh fruit with the natural yoghurt.
2 Sweeten to taste if necessary with a little honey.
3 Serve in individual dishes.

CHILDREN'S FUN FEASTS

PARTY PASTA AND TRIANGLE SALAD WITH FRUIT JUICE

Here are some fun food feasts for young children to help you win the mealtime battle!

Serves 4   £££

SHOPPING LIST

2 punnets mustard and cress
4 tomatoes
1 large carrot
fruit juice of choice
2 slices lean ham
4 triangular cheese spreads

TIME PLAN

1   Cook pasta.
2   Prepare and arrange salad, clear decks.
3   Drain the pasta and follow complete party pasta recipe.
4   Serve feast.

▶ PARTY PASTA

8 oz (225 g) dried pasta shapes
1 teaspoon Marmite mixed with
   1 tablespoon sunflower oil

2 slices lean ham
2 punnets mustard and cress, washed

1   Cook the pasta in boiling water for 8 to 10 minutes.
2   Drain the pasta and return it to the saucepan.
3   Add the Marmite and oil, mix and toss well together.
4   Scatter over the ham and mustard and cress.
5   Serve straight away with the triangle salad.

► TRIANGLE SALAD

4 triangular cheese spreads, split
  in half
4 tomatoes, thinly sliced

1 large carrot, grated
fruit juice of choice

1 Arrange the tomato and cheese slices alternately on a large plate.
2 Scatter with grated carrot.
3 Serve with fruit juice.

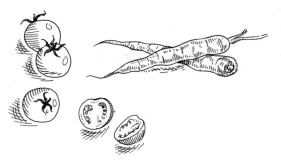

FISHY PIZZAS

BANANA COCKTAIL

Serves 4   £££

SHOPPING LIST

4 oz (100 g) mushrooms
2 tomatoes
4 small ripe bananas
2 × 4½-oz (120-g) tins sardines in
  tomato sauce
1 × 7-oz (200-g) tin fruit cocktail
  in natural juice
4 wholemeal pitta breads
2 oz (50 g) Edam cheese
5 fl oz (150 ml) fromage frais

TIME PLAN

1 Follow stages 1 to 5 of fishy
    pizza recipe (overleaf).
2 Prepare banana cocktail
    (overleaf) and set to one
    side.
3 Heat baked beans.
4 Serve pizzas and beans.
5 Serve banana cocktail when
    ready.

▶ FISHY PIZZAS

4 wholemeal pitta breads
2 × 4½-oz (120-g) tins sardines in
   tomato sauce
4 oz (100 g) mushrooms, sliced
2 tomatoes, sliced

2 oz (50 g) Edam cheese, grated
1 teaspoon dried oregano
1 × 14-oz (400-g) tin beans in
   tomato sauce

1   Pre-heat the grill.
2   Lightly toast the pitta breads on each side.
3   In a small bowl, mash the sardines.
4   Spread one side of the pitta breads with the sardine mixture. Scatter
    over the sliced mushrooms. Arrange tomato slices over the top and
    sprinkle with the grated cheese and oregano.
5   Place under the hot grill for 4 to 5 minutes until bubbling hot and
    golden.
6   Serve with hot beans in tomato sauce.

▶ BANANA COCKTAIL

4 small ripe bananas
5 fl oz (150 ml) fromage frais
1 × 7-oz (200-g) tin fruit cocktail
   in natural juice

4 teaspoons runny honey
1 teaspoon ground cinnamon

1   Peel the bananas, split them in half lengthways and lay each split
    banana in a serving dish.
2   Slit each banana half lengthwise to open it up and fill with fromage
    frais.
3   Spoon over the fruit cocktail and drizzle over the honey.
4   Sprinkle with cinnamon and serve.

SUPER SEEDY CRUMBLE

PINEAPPLE SLUSH

Children love to cook, so be brave – get them into the kitchen to help make these mouth-watering feasts.

Serves 4 £££

SHOPPING LIST

1 onion
4 oz (100 g) mushrooms
4 oz (100 g) frozen runner beans
1 × 14-oz (400-g) tin crushed
   pineapple in natural juice
4 slices wholemeal bread
2 oz (50 g) Cheddar cheese
10 fl oz (300 ml) natural yoghurt

TIME PLAN

1   Follow stage 1 of pineapple
    slush recipe (overleaf).
2   Follow stages 1 to 6 of
    crumble recipe.
3   Spoon pineapple slush into
    glasses and sprinkle with
    topping.
4   Remove crumble from grill.
5   Serve feast.

▶ **SUPER SEEDY CRUMBLE**

1 onion, grated
1 teaspoon garlic purée
4 oz (100 g) mushrooms, sliced
4 oz (100 g) frozen runner beans
1 × 14-oz (400-g) tin beans in
   tomato sauce
freshly ground black pepper

For the crumble topping
4 oz (100 g) porridge oats
2 oz (50 g) peanuts, chopped
3 tablespoons sunflower seeds
2 oz (50 g) Cheddar cheese,
   grated
1 tablespoon sunflower oil

4 slices wholemeal bread
butter or margarine for spreading

103

1   Pre-heat the grill.
2   Dry fry the onion and garlic purée over a gentle heat until soft (about 1
    to 2 minutes).
3   Stir in the mushrooms and cook for a few minutes until they begin to
    soften. Add the runner beans and tinned beans and bring to the boil,
    then simmer, covered, for 4 to 5 minutes. Season to taste with black
    pepper.
4   For the crumble, mix all the ingredients together and set to one side.
5   Pour the bean mixture into a shallow flameproof dish.
6   Scatter over the crumble mixture and place under the hot grill for 3 to
    4 minutes.
7   Serve with wholemeal bread and butter.

► PINEAPPLE SLUSH

1 × 14-oz (400-g) tin crushed   *For the topping*
   pineapple in natural juice   1 tablespoon dark brown sugar
10 fl oz (300 ml) natural yoghurt   1 teaspoon ground ginger

1   Carefully fold together the crushed pineapple and yoghurt. Pour this
    mixture into a large shallow freezerproof dish. Place in the freezer for
    10 to 12 minutes.
2   Spoon the pineapple slush into 4 glasses and sprinkle with the brown
    sugar and ginger topping.

CHEESY CORN COBS WITH SARDINE BAGUETTE

ORANGE COOLERS

Serves 4   £££££

SHOPPING LIST

4 corn on the cob
4 oranges
2 × 4½-oz (120-g) tins sardines in tomato sauce
1 large brown French stick
2 oz (50 g) Cheddar cheese
2 oz (50 g) low fat cream cheese

TIME PLAN

1   Follow stage 1 of corn cob recipe.
2   Prepare orange coolers and freeze. Clear decks.
3   Follow stages 1 to 4 of baguette recipe (overleaf).
4   Follow stages 2 to 4 of corn cob recipe.
5   Serve feast.

▶ ## CHEESY CORN COBS

4 corn on the cob   2 oz (50 g) Cheddar, grated
1 oz (25 g) butter   1 teaspoon French mustard

1   Cook the corn in boiling water for 10 to 12 minutes, or until tender.
2   Meanwhile, beat the butter, cheese and mustard together.
3   Drain the corn, place one cob of corn on each plate and spread with the cheese mixture.
4   Serve at once with sardine baguette.

► SARDINE BAGUETTE

2 × 4½-oz (120-g) tins sardines in
tomato sauce
2 oz (50 g) low fat cream cheese
freshly ground black pepper

1 teaspoon garlic purée
1 teaspoon dried thyme
1 large brown French stick

1 Pre-heat the oven to 425°F (220°C), gas mark 7.
2 Mash the sardines in a bowl with the cream cheese, black pepper, garlic
   purée and dried thyme.
3 Using a sharp knife, slice the French bread almost all the way through
   so that it is still attached at the base. Open and spread the sardine mixture between the slices and press the slices back together again.
4 Place the bread on a baking tray and bake in the oven for 8 to 10
   minutes. Serve hot.

► ORANGE COOLERS

See recipe on page 30.

Some Great Sandwich and Picnic Ideas

Here is a collection of hot and cold sandwich and picnic feasts. They are quick, filling and very tasty – none of them will take longer than 15 minutes. What more could you ask for?

Pitta Toasts with Chick Pea Butter

Serves 4   £

For the chick pea butter
1 × 15-oz (425-g) tin chick peas, drained
1 tablespoon lemon juice
1 tablespoon sunflower oil
2 teaspoons ground coriander
1 teaspoon garlic purée

4 to 5 tablespoons hot water
freshly ground black pepper

4 wholemeal pitta breads
cayenne pepper
2 punnets mustard and cress

1   First make the chick pea butter. In a bowl, simply mash with a fork or liquidise the ingredients together well. Season with black pepper.
2   Heat the grill and toast the pitta breads on both sides. Split in half while still hot, spread the untoasted side with the chick pea butter. Sprinkle with a little cayenne pepper and place under the grill for 2 to 3 minutes until bubbling hot. Serve at once scattered with the mustard and cress.

Variation
Alternatively, grill the split untoasted sides of the pitta breads and serve hot with a bowl of the chick pea butter.

PITTA POCKET FEASTS

Delicious to take on a picnic or to eat as a quick filling snack.

Serves 4   £££

2 punnets mustard and cress
1 × 14-oz (400-g) tin butter
  beans, drained
8 oz (225 g) sprouted mung
  beans
2 sticks celery, chopped
2 large carrots, grated
1 × 7-oz (200-g) tin sweetcorn,
  drained
4 oz (100 g) peanuts
freshly ground black pepper

For the yoghurt dressing
5 fl oz (150 ml) natural yoghurt
1 teaspoon mint sauce
1 teaspoon garlic purée
2 teaspoons tomato purée
1 tablespoon soy sauce
freshly ground black pepper

4 wholemeal pitta breads

1   In a large mixing bowl, combine the salad ingredients together. Season
    to taste with black pepper.
2   In a small bowl, beat together dressing ingredients and season to taste
    with black pepper. Drizzle the dressing over the tossed salad and mix
    well.
3   Cut each pitta bread in half, open the pockets and stuff well with the
    salad.

SARDINE DOUBLE DECKER

Serves 4   £

4 wholemeal baps
3 × 4½-oz (120-g) tins sardines in
  tomato sauce
2 teaspoons wholegrain mustard
1 teaspoon dried mixed herbs

1 teaspoon garlic purée
freshly ground black pepper
4 large tomatoes, sliced
1 bunch watercress, picked over
  and washed

1   Slice each bap into three and set the bap tops to one side.
2   In a bowl, mash the sardines, mustard, mixed herbs, garlic purée and
    black pepper together.
3   Spread the sardine pâté over the bap slices and arrange tomato slices
    and watercress on top.
4   Sandwich the baps together and top each decker with the reserved
    lids. Place each decker on a plate and tuck in!

VEGETABLE PITTA DIP

Serve this dip as a light lunch or supper dish or wrap it and take it on a picnic.

Serves 4 £££

For the dip
2 red apples, washed, cored and
   finely diced
1 tablespoon lemon juice
6 oz (175 g) low fat cream cheese
   or curd cheese
2 teaspoons tandoori or tikka
   paste
1 small onion, grated
2 oz (50 g) raisins or sultanas
freshly ground black pepper

Selection of raw vegetables cut
   into sticks, such as carrots,
   celery, cauliflower florets and
   cucumber
4 wholemeal pitta breads, cut
   into fingers

1   Place all the dip ingredients in a bowl and mix together. Season to taste with black pepper.
2   Spoon the dip into a serving bowl and place in the centre of a large plate.
3   Surround the dip with the vegetables and pitta bread fingers.

APPLE AND WALNUT PAN BAGNA

Pan bagna is a sandwich which originates from the Mediterranean. The bread is usually rubbed with fresh garlic and the ingredients vary depending on what is in season.

Serves 4   £££

1 large brown French stick
2 large cloves garlic, crushed
1 tablespoon sunflower oil
6 oz (175 g) curd cheese
2 oz (50 g) Cheddar or blue
    cheese
2 sticks celery, chopped

2 red apples, cored and sliced
4 oz (100 g) walnut halves
1 tablespoon fromage frais
freshly ground black pepper
3 large carrots, grated
¼ cos or Webb's lettuce

1   Split the French stick in half lengthways. Mix the crushed garlic and oil together and brush and rub over the cut side of the bread halves.
2   Beat together the cheeses, celery, apples, walnuts and fromage frais. Season with black pepper. Spread the cheese mixture over one half of the bread and scatter over the grated carrots. Add the crisp lettuce leaves and sandwich together with the remaining half of the French stick. Press firmly together.
3   Serve cut into 4 pieces or wrap in kitchen foil and pack for a picnic.

TUNA ON RYE

Serves 4   £££

1 × 6-oz (175-g) tin tuna fish in
   brine, drained
1 tablespoon lemon juice
1 bunch spring onions, chopped
8 oz (225 g) cottage cheese
freshly ground black pepper

crisp lettuce leaves
4 thick slices rye bread
4 oz (100 g) black grapes, halved
   and deseeded
1 bunch radishes, washed and
   thickly sliced

1   In a mixing bowl, fork together the tuna fish, lemon juice, spring
    onions and cottage cheese. Season with black pepper.
2   Arrange the crisp lettuce leaves on the rye bread and carefully pile on
    the tuna mix. Place the halved grapes on top and scatter over the sliced
    radishes.

OPEN SESAME

Here are some ideas for open sandwiches.

▶ BANANA MUNCH

Serves 4   £

4 tablespoons crunchy peanut
   butter
¼ cucumber, finely diced
freshly ground black pepper
4 thick slices granary bread

2 ripe bananas, sliced
1 × 7-oz (200-g) tin mandarin
   segments in natural juice,
   drained
2 punnets mustard and cress

1   In a small mixing bowl, beat together the peanut butter and diced
    cucumber and season to taste with black pepper.
2   Spread the nut butter over the granary bread and carefully arrange
    the sliced bananas and mandarin segments over the top. Scatter with
    mustard and cress and serve.

▶ AVOCADO MELT

Grilled avocado toastie – mmmmmmm delicious!

Serves 4   £££

4 thick slices wholemeal bread
2 ripe avocadoes
1 tablespoon lemon juice
1 tablespoon Worcestershire
  sauce

1 small onion, grated
freshly ground black pepper
4 tomatoes, sliced
3 oz (75 g) bean sprouts
3 oz (75 g) Edam cheese, grated

1   Toast the bread lightly on each side.
2   In a small mixing bowl, mash the avocadoes, lemon juice,
    Worcestershire sauce, grated onion and black pepper. Spread this
    mixture over the toasted bread.
3   Place the sliced tomatoes over the top and scatter on a handful of bean
    sprouts. Scatter with the grated Edam cheese and return to the grill for
    a further 2 to 3 minutes until golden brown.
4   Finish with freshly ground black pepper and serve at once.

SPEEDY PUDS

FRUITY BRULÉE

It is important to use demerara sugar for this recipe as this helps form a good crust for your fruit brulée. Frozen fruit makes a good alternative.

Serves 4 £££

12 oz (350 g) fresh fruit such as strawberries, peaches, raspberries, apricots

10 fl oz (300 ml) thick set natural or Greek yoghurt
4 tablespoons demerara sugar

1 Pre-heat the grill.
2 Prepare and cut the fruit into small pieces. Divide between 4 flameproof ramekin dishes or place all the mixture in a small soufflé or flameproof dish.
3 Spoon and carefully spread the yoghurt over the fruit. Sprinkle and cover the yoghurt with the demerara sugar.
4 Place under the hot grill for approximately 2 minutes until the sugar bubbles and gets a good golden brown colour – but watch carefully as sugar burns easily.
5 Serve straight from the grill, or alternatively, chill and serve cold.

GINGERNUT TRIFLE

Fromage frais is a wonderful ingredient, low in fat and not as sharp as natural yoghurt. It makes a great substitute for cream.

Serves 4   £££

12 gingernut biscuits
4 oz (100 g) breakfast muesli
1 × 14-oz (400-g) tin peaches in
  natural juice
1 pint (600 ml) fromage frais
1 teaspoon vanilla essence

zest of 1 orange
4 oz (100 g) white grapes, halved
  and deseeded
4 oz (100 g) black grapes, halved
  and deseeded
1 tablespoon brown sugar

1   Crush the gingernut biscuits in a saucepan using the end of a rolling pin. Mix in the breakfast muesli and spoon into a trifle dish.
2   Pour the tin of peaches and juice over the top of the biscuit mix.
3   In a small bowl, mix the fromage frais with the vanilla essence and orange zest. Spoon this mixture over the peaches, using the back of the spoon carefully to cover the biscuit mix with the cream.
4   Decorate with the halved grapes and sprinkle with brown sugar.

HOT MULLED NECTARINES
WITH HAZELNUT CREAM

A delicious and warming dish – peaches can be used as an alternative.
When nectarines and peaches are not in season, pears make a great substitute but they must be ripe.

Serves 4   £££

6 ripe nectarines

For the syrup
1 × 7-oz (200-g) tin frozen
  concentrated orange juice
1 bay leaf
1 teaspoon mixed spice
2 teaspoons runny honey
10 fl oz (300 ml) water

For the hazelnut cream
4 oz (100 g) low fat cream or
  curd cheese
4 oz (100 g) hazelnuts, chopped
5 fl oz (150 ml) fromage frais

1   Split the nectarines in half and remove the stones. Place them in
    a saucepan with the syrup ingredients, bring to the boil, cover and
    simmer for 7 minutes.
2   In a small bowl, beat together the cream or curd cheese and hazelnuts,
    carefully mix in the fromage frais and spoon into a serving dish.
3   Spoon the mulled nectarines into an attractive dish and serve with the
    hazelnut cream.

BANANA SOUFFLÉ SURPRISE

Soufflés are really easy to make – don't be put off by the grand name. For this soufflé omelette you will need a large non-stick frying pan.

Serves 4   £££

4 eggs, separated
2 tablespoons desiccated coconut
2 large bananas, peeled and
  chopped

1 tablespoon sunflower oil
1 × 7-oz (200-g) tin raspberries in
  natural juice
2 teaspoons ground cinnamon

1   Pre-heat the grill.
2   In a medium-size bowl, beat together the egg yolks and desiccated coconut until pale. Fold in the chopped bananas.
3   In a large dry mixing bowl, whisk the egg whites until stiff. Heat the oil in a large frying pan until hot. Meanwhile, using a large spoon, carefully fold the whisked egg whites into the banana mixture.
4   Pour the soufflé mixture into the hot frying pan and cook for 3 to 4 minutes until the mixture sets.
5   Place the pan under the hot grill for a further 2 to 3 minutes or until puffed and golden brown.
6   To serve, spoon over the raspberries and juice, sprinkle with cinnamon and serve straight from the pan.

PEAR AND LOGANBERRY PANCAKE PIE

A lovely combination of fruits, cream cheese and chocolate pancakes.

Serves 4   £££

For the batter
2 oz (50 g) wholemeal flour
1 tablespoon cocoa powder
1 egg
5 fl oz (150 ml) semi-skimmed
milk
1 tablespoon sunflower oil

For the filling
1 lb (450 g) ripe William pears,
cored and sliced
1 teaspoon ground cinnamon
1 × 7-oz (200-g) tin loganberries
in natural juice
1 tablespoon brown sugar
4 oz (100 g) low fat cream cheese
10 fl oz (300 ml) natural yoghurt
vanilla essence to taste
a little oil for greasing

1   In a large bowl, beat together the flour, cocoa, egg, milk and oil; beat well until smooth.
2   Heat a non-stick frying pan. Add a little oil and wipe out with kitchen paper. Pour a quarter of the batter into the pan, just enough to coat the base. Cook for 1 minute, loosen the edge with a round-bladed knife, then turn the pancake over and cook the other side. Continue until you have 4 pancakes.
3   Mix together the sliced pears, cinnamon and loganberries, juice and brown sugar.
4   Mix together the cream cheese and yoghurt. Add a few drops of vanilla essence to taste.
5   To assemble the pancake pie, put the first pancake on a plate. Spread with a thin layer of the cream cheese mixture and fruit, cover with a second pancake and repeat with the remaining pancakes. Spoon over the remaining cream cheese mixture and fruit.
6   Chill for 1 hour and serve cut into wedges.

DECORATIVE FRUIT PLATTER

A stunning way to present fruit; any combination may be used.

Serves 4   £££

1 × 14-oz (400-g) tin apricots in natural juice

Suggested fruit
2 passion fruit
4 oz (100 g) black grapes, halved and deseeded

2 kiwi fruit, peeled and each sliced into 4
1 banana, peeled and sliced on a slant
8 strawberries, washed

1   Liquidise the tin of apricots with their juice until smooth.
2   Prepare the fruits.
3   Using a teaspoon, scoop out the flesh from the passion fruit into a cup and set to one side.
4   Spoon the apricot sauce over the surface of 4 large dinner plates.
5   Carefully arrange the fruit on the apricot sauce in an attractive pattern.
6   Spoon the passion fruit pulp over the banana slices and serve.

THE FAST BAKE-IN

SPRING ONION AND HAZELNUT SHORTBREAD

This tasty shortbread goes well with soups, stews and salads.

Makes 12 shortbread fingers   £

6 oz (175 g) wholemeal self-
  raising flour
3 oz (75 g) sunflower margarine
½ bunch spring onions, chopped

2 oz (50 g) hazelnuts, chopped
2 teaspoons paprika
1 tablespoon cold water
extra paprika for sprinkling

1   Pre-heat the oven to 400°F (200°C), gas mark 6. Lightly flour a baking tray and set to one side.
2   In a large mixing bowl, rub together the flour and sunflower margarine until the mixture resembles coarse breadcrumbs.
3   Add the spring onions, hazelnuts, paprika and water to the breadcrumb mixture and bind together.
4   Roll out on to the prepared baking tray into a large rectangle. Neaten the edges with a knife and mark into 12 shortbread fingers. Prick over the surface with a fork and sprinkle with paprika.
5   Bake for 10 minutes until lightly coloured.

ORANGE AND CINNAMON COOKIES

These speedy biscuits are excellent served with fruit puddings or with a pot of tea.

Makes 18 biscuits   £

4 oz (100 g) sunflower margarine
2 oz (50 g) muscovado sugar
grated rind of 1 orange

5 oz (150 g) self-raising
    wholemeal flour
3 teaspoons ground cinnamon
icing sugar for dusting

1   Pre-heat the oven to 400°F (200°C), gas mark 6.
2   In a mixing bowl, cream together the margarine, sugar and orange rind.
3   Sift in the flour and cinnamon and mix well.
4   Roll the mixture with your hands into walnut-size pieces and place on a lightly floured baking tray.
5   Flatten the cookies with a wet fork and bake for 8 to 10 minutes.
6   Allow to cool slightly before transferring on to a wire rack.
7   Dust with icing sugar when cool.

PEANUT AND APRICOT MELTS

Peanut butter and apricots make a delicious addition to these muesli cookies.

Makes 18 melts £

2 oz (50 g) sunflower margarine
1 oz (25 g) brown sugar
1 oz (25 g) crunchy peanut butter
1 small egg

1½ oz (40 g) self-raising wholemeal flour
3 oz (75 g) breakfast muesli
2 oz (50 g) dried apricots, chopped

1   Pre-heat the oven to 425°F (220°C), gas mark 7.
2   In a mixing bowl, beat together the margarine, brown sugar and peanut butter. Gradually beat in the egg. Tip all the dried ingredients into the mixture and carefully fold in.
3   Spoon the mixture on to 2 lightly greased baking sheets. With the back of the spoon, spread each spoonful into a thin round, allowing space between each as they will spread a little.
4   Bake for approximately 10 minutes until lightly coloured.
5   Cool on a wire rack.

SUPER SEEDY BROWNIES

The combination of seeds in these brownies adds extra flavour and nutrients.

Makes 12 brownies £

4 oz (100 g) sunflower margarine
1 oz (25 g) cocoa powder
4 oz (100 g) brown sugar
2 eggs
a few drops vanilla essence
2 oz (50 g) self-raising wholemeal
   flour

1 banana, chopped
1 oz (25 g) sunflower seeds
1 oz (25 g) sesame seeds
icing sugar to decorate
sunflower oil for greasing

1   Pre-heat the oven to 425°F (220°C), gas mark 7.
2   Lightly grease a sheet of greaseproof paper with sunflower oil and line a Swiss roll or roasting tin.
3   In a saucepan, melt the margarine over a gentle heat. Remove from the heat and add the cocoa powder.
4   In a large mixing bowl, beat together the sugar, eggs and vanilla essence.
5   Using a large spoon, quickly fold the flour, seeds and chopped banana into the beaten mixture.
6   Pour the mixture into the prepared tin and spread evenly.
7   Bake in the oven for approximately 10 minutes.
8   To serve, cut into squares and dust with icing sugar.

MEXICAN CORN AND CHILLI BREAD

These corn and chilli breads are excellent to serve as an accompaniment to main meals or great for snacks and picnics.

Makes 8 £

4 oz (100 g) self-raising
  wholemeal flour
4 oz (100 g) self-raising flour
½ teaspoon bicarbonate of soda
1 teaspoon chilli powder

1 × 7-oz (200-g) tin sweetcorn
1 tablespoon tikka paste
8 fl oz (250 ml) natural yoghurt
sunflower oil for frying

1 Mix the flours, bicarbonate of soda and chilli powder together. Add the sweetcorn, tikka paste and yoghurt and mix to soft dough.
2 Turn the dough out on to a floured table top and divide into 8 pieces.
3 Using your hands, pat out each piece of dough into a round the size of a saucer.
4 Heat a teaspoonful of sunflower oil in the frying pan until hot. Fry each corn bread for 1 to 2 minutes on each side, cooking 2 at a time. The corn bread should puff up slightly.
5 Keep the corn bread wrapped in a warm napkin or clean tea towel to keep it warm ready for serving.

INDEX